GET REAL!

A STUDENT'S GUIDE TO MONEY
& OTHER PRACTICAL MATTERS

JAMES TENUTO & SUSAN SCHWARTZWALD

Illustrated by Andrea Dietrich

HBJ

A HARVEST/HBJ ORIGINAL

HARCOURT BRACE JOVANOVICH, PUBLISHERS

San Diego   New York   London

Library of Congress Cataloging-in-Publication Data

Tenuto, James, 1953-
  Get real! : a student's guide to money and other practical matters / by James Tenuto and Susan Schwartzwald.
    p.   cm.
ISBN 0-15-600595-6
1. Youth—Finance, Personal. 2. Teenagers as consumers. 3. Young adults—Finance, Personal. I. Schwartzwald, Susan, 1956- . II. Title
HG179.T42 1992
332.024'055—dc20   91-23641
                                                              CIP

Designed by G. B. D. Smith

Printed in the United States of America

First Edition

A B C D E

CONTENTS

▼ ▼ ▼

ACKNOWLEDGMENTS

We want to thank everyone who helped make *Get Real!* a reality. Most of all, we are grateful to those individuals—both corporate and academic—who agreed to be interviewed for this book. Because these experts have generously shared their experiences with us, our readers will have an easier time adjusting to real-world complexities.

In addition, we extend special thanks to everyone who had a hands-on role in the development of this book. We are grateful to Lynn Tenuto for her good humor, patience, and support; to Myra C. Strauss for her editorial skill; and to David Lipkin for his legal advice. We also thank Andrea Dietrich, who created our wonderful illustrations, and G. B. D. Smith, who designed a cover more striking than we could have imagined.

Finally, we think our book is as good as it looks. For that, we owe many thanks to our editor at HBJ, Emily Thompson.

CHECKS AND
BALANCES

▼ ▼ ▼

*Like many of us, my Aunt Kay had always been a bit intimidated
by banks. "I'd been banking for 25 years, but I was never comfortable when I walked into a bank," she reminisced. "In a supermarket I could always tell what line to stand in, but I never knew
which of the five lines at the bank to stand in until I'd waited 10
minutes in one . . . and then I'd be politely told to try again, 'over
there.' And there never seemed to be a receptionist at a bank!
When I had a question a teller couldn't handle, I was forced to
wander from desk to desk seeking help, all the while feeling myself
get smaller and smaller."*

Aunt Kay found her own solution to these problems. She became a banker!

Bankers aren't really rude or unfriendly, but they often look that way. Bankers are in charge of money, so they want to project an image of trustworthiness, security, and probity. They achieve this image by creating an air of formality and physical distance . . . stodginess. Notice how bankers dress. There's not a hightop to be seen, nor dangling watermelon earrings, nor a rainbow-colored hairdo. Everyone at a bank, from teller to president, is conservative- and professional-looking. There's a reason for this. Most people feel a lot better turning their money over to someone who appears to know what to do with it.

But bankers have to deal with more than money; they also have to deal with people. In fact, they want to deal with *you*. Banking is, after all, a *service* industry. You should expect and receive that service. So don't lose your confidence when you walk through those glass doors.

For many, opening a checking account at a bank is their first independent financial responsibility. A checking account is really just an efficient way to keep and spend money. Since it keeps your money both safe and accessible, it can be a necessity on any campus. So how do you begin this first banking relationship? Let's walk through some of the how-to's.

Choosing the Bank

How do you select a bank that will be right for you? One way to chose is to stick with what you know. You might, for instance, want to open your account at a branch of the bank where your family already does business. Then your parents could make automatic deposits into your account at their local branch. If your family's bank doesn't have branches near you, you might rely on what your friends know. For instance, you could ask a junior or senior at your new school which nearby banks she would recommend.

Many schools hold a "Bank Day" early in the fall semester or first quarter. Find out if your school does. Bank representatives attend Bank Days to discuss the services and products each of their institutions has to offer. Talking with the representatives of several banks is a good way to "shop" for a bank.

When shopping for a bank, you're trying to find out what particular advantages a specific bank can offer you. And while you're shopping, keep these points in mind:

CONVENIENCE Is the bank close to school or your apartment? Are there branches located around town? Is there an Automatic Teller Machine (ATM) or Money Access Center (MAC) available?

TYPES OF ACCOUNTS OFFERED Does the bank cater to individuals or businesses? Will you earn interest on your checking account? Do you need to maintain a minimum balance? Will you get a credit card along with your account? What are the fees?

SPECIAL OFFERINGS Will you get a free toaster—or a free anything—if you open an account with a particular bank?

FUTURE BUSINESS Will this bank be able to handle your future needs, such as car loans and savings?

Why do banks send representatives to college campuses in search of student checking accounts? According to Laura Morefield, Assistant Vice President, District Sales, and Service Manager of First Interstate Bank in California, the college student opening his first account represents a "potential lifetime customer for the bank." Your savings account, business accounts, home mortgage, and retirement accounts may all be provided by the same bank that opened your first checking account. Recognize your worth!

What to Bring

Money . . .

To open a checking account at a bank, you must first deposit funds in the form of cash or a cash substitute—traveler's checks, a cashier's check, or a personal check.

Cash is cash—pennies, nickels, dimes, quarters . . . and greenbacks in all denominations. Cash is good anywhere, any time, and all banks accept it.

Traveler's checks are issued by most banks and offer merchants—and other banks—a guarantee that the money is "good." Traveler's checks, then, are as good as cash to the bank. To you, traveler's checks are better than cash. If they're lost or stolen, you can replace them.

A cashier's check is a check issued by a bank and drawn on its own funds; like traveler's checks, it guarantees "good money." You don't need to have an account at a bank to get a cashier's check. You can purchase one with cash. Banks typically honor other banks' cashier's checks. Sometimes, however, a bank will place a "hold" on a cashier's check. This simply means that the check must pass through the bank's clearinghouse. If the cashier's check you deposit comes from a bank that shares the same clearinghouse as your new bank, the funds should clear in two days. But, if the banks use different clearinghouses and the banks are in different parts of the country, it can take as long as nine days for a cashier's check to clear. Thus, while some banks will treat your cashier's check as ready money, you should be prepared to wait. Have an emergency reserve of cash or traveler's checks to tide you over until the bank clears your check. You can determine a reasonable reserve by estimating the costs of getting established . . . paying for meals, stocking the fridge, going to a movie, and so on.

Personal checks, however, are not considered cash. Though banks often will accept them to open an account, they may delay the use of these funds until it's been determined that the check is good. (Why? Because people have been known to write checks without having any money in their accounts.)

ID as in Identification

Surprisingly, money alone is not enough to open your account. You also have to prove that you are *you*. So, you must also bring at least two pieces of identification. Laura Morefield of First Interstate suggests two photo IDs—that is, IDs with your picture on them. These can include a passport, a driver's license, a current academic year student identification, or a non-driver's license ID (provided by most states' Department of Motor Vehicles). Not acceptable are a Social Security card, library card, or birth certificate. Some banks will honor an acceptance letter from your university or college in lieu of a valid student ID, especially if you are an early registrant. Others won't.

There's one surefire way to check on what ID your bank requires before you get there: call and ask. Having the right ID will help you make a good impression at your first meeting with a bank—and it'll save you a second trip.

Types of Checking Accounts

You'll find that every bank offers slightly different services and charges different fees. Generally, you'll be charged a monthly fee for the account. Some banks have a per-check charge—usually 15 to 50 cents per check. Others may give you free checking if you maintain a minimum balance in your account. In addition, you'll more than likely receive an automatic teller card to use at an automatic teller machine (ATM). The bank may also offer special services. Some institutions, for instance, offer credit services such as overdraft protection and/or a credit card tied directly to your account. Usually, however, the more services you have tied to your account, the higher the fees.

Each bank offers an array of checking accounts, and each account has its own unique features, benefits, and costs. To make a suitable choice, sit down with the new accounts clerk and tell him or her what your situation is and what your needs are. Don't be afraid to ask questions—and keep asking until you're sure you understand the answers. You may discover that you "need" unlimited checking (the ability to write a large number of checks without a per-check fee). Or, you may "need" overdraft protection, which means the bank will honor a check you've written even if you've temporarily run out of money in your account.

Let's look at a couple of banks to see what features and services can be offered.

New York–based Citibank has special programs for college students and has designed an account for them. Lilieth Taylor, Assistant Vice President, who heads up this banking unit, recommends the "Citi-One" account. If you maintain $3000 in any combination of Citibank accounts, no fees are charged in the Citi-One account. Otherwise, you can expect to pay $12.00 per month and 25 cents per check. A "budget" checking account costs $4.00 per month with no per-check charges, but you're limited to six transactions per month.

Citi-One also provides credit services as part of this account. Should you write a check for more than the balance in your account, your overdraft protection allows the bank to honor the check essentially by extending a line of credit—a temporary loan—to you. This sounds good, but there's a catch: you must pay this money back, and the rate of interest you'll pay on an overdraft loan is often high—usually credit-card rates of 12% to 19.6%. Citi-One also offers a credit card, a Mastercard or Visa, which will allow you to master the possibilities of a $500 credit limit. The requirements for a credit card are simple. You don't have to be employed, but you should have no negative reports in your credit file. This credit file, or history, is commonly referred to as your "bureau," after the credit bureaus, or companies, that keep the records of who's paying their bills and who's not.

Citibank also offers two interest-earning savings accounts: one an insured money-market account, and the other a "day-to-day" fixed-rate account. *Money-market funds* earn interest at a rate that fluctuates daily, depending upon current market conditions. A *fixed-rate account* earns interest at a predetermined minimum rate, say 5.25%. Limited check writing with no minimum balance is one feature of these accounts.

Now let's head to the West Coast and see what the venerable Bank of America (BofA) has to offer. Like Citicorp, BofA also wants college students to open checking accounts. Rich Martino, checking account product manager of BofA, recommends a flat-fee checking account for college students. For $6.00 a month you can write as many checks as you like; there's no per-check charge and you don't have to maintain a minimum balance. You also get the Versatel card, BofA's ATM card, as part of this flat-fee account.

As an alternative for those who don't use their accounts very much, he recommends BofA's Limited Checking Account, which—for a $3.50 service charge—offers up to eight free checks and eight free ATM withdrawals each month. There's no minimum balance requirement on this account either.

Bank of America also offers a credit card, a Visa or Master-Card, but its criteria are a bit more stringent than those of Citibank. The student must meet six requirements to receive this credit card with a $500 limit. You must—

1. Be at least 18 years old.
2. Be a U.S. citizen.
3. Be enrolled as a full-time junior or senior at a qualified four-year accredited college, or as a graduate student.
4. Have a history as a good checking account customer for six months.
5. Have at least $200 verifiable monthly income after tuition, rent, utilities, and food expenses are paid.
6. Have a satisfactory credit history.

Like Citicorp, Bank of America also offers fixed-rate savings accounts and money-market accounts that let you write checks and earn interest.

These are examples of the types of accounts available at two very large banks. The services these banks offer and the fees they charge are fairly typical. But smaller, local banks in each town may offer different services worth considering. Try visiting at least two different banks to see what each has to offer. Then choose the one that suits you.

Pick the bank that best fits your needs. How many checks will you be writing each month? Is the ATM a critical factor? Can you meet the minimum-balance requirement to get the fees waived? How do you want to be treated when you walk in? Select your bank or savings institution carefully, for you, too, may be picking a "lifetime partner."

Checks and Balances

You've selected your bank and opened an account; now you're ready for business. Follow this simple rule and you'll never go wrong (at least, not broke): **Don't write checks for more money than you have in your account.** First of all, it's illegal. You've heard of rubber checks? That's what overdrafts are—checks that "bounce" back to you because you don't have enough money in your account to cover them. Second, it can be expensive. A bounced check can cost you anywhere from $10 to $30. *(Note:* The bank and the merchant both charge you for the rubber check!) Even if you have overdraft protection, try not to exceed in spending what you have available in the account. Remember that you have to pay back the amount of the overdraft, usually with interest.

More than likely, your personal credit history, or "bureau," will include information on how you handle your checking account. This is another reason for avoiding overdrafts. Establish that good credit history right from the start. A good, solid reputation with a bank will help you tremendously in such future endeavors as getting a consumer loan, a car loan, or a mortgage.

How can you make sure you don't blow it and write a bad check by accident? Simple. Just keep track of your funds by balancing, or *reconciling,* your monthly statement. The bank's customer services representative will show you how to do this. Every month, your bank will send you a record—or *statement*—of all the transactions you've made during the previous month. (Some banks even send your canceled checks.) When you receive the statement, compare it with your own records, which are listed in your *check register.* Most banks offer brochures that take you through a sample check register and demonstrate how to balance the statement.

		RECORD ALL CHARGES OR CREDITS THAT AFFECT YOUR ACCOUNT			√	FEE (IF ANY) (-)	DEPOSIT/CREDIT (+)	BALANCE	
NUMBER	DATE	DESCRIPTION OF TRANSACTION	PAYMENT/DEBIT (-)		T			$ 175	65
127	3/8	GAP	$ 17	83		,25	$	18	08
								157	57
128	3/11	Buck's Ticket Agency	32	50		.25		32	75
								124	82
ATM	3/14	Withdrawal ATM	20	00		—		20	00
								104	82
	3/15	Deposit Paycheck					151 07	151	07
								255	89
129	3/20	Allstate Insurance	$5	00		.25		85	25
								170	64
130	3/25	Acme Market	16	79		.25		17	04
								153	60
	3/30	Monthly fee	6	00		—		6	00
								147	60
	3/30	Deposit Paycheck					151 07	151	07
								298	67
131	4/4	Mastercard	102	43		.25		102	68
								195	99
	4/5	Deposit: Income Tax Refund	— —				202 00	202	00
								397	99
132	4/7	Domino's Pizza	8	88		.25		9	13
								388	86
133	4/8	Bookstore - Get Real	12	95		.25		13	20
								375	66

REMEMBER TO RECORD AUTOMATIC PAYMENTS / DEPOSITS ON DATE AUTHORIZED.

The check register is that thing you keep in your checkbook along with the checks. This is where you make your entries. One sure way of not messing up your checking account is to make all your entries—checks, withdrawals, and deposits—when you make the transaction. Take a look at the sample check register above. There are columns to record a check number, the date, and a description of the transaction, columns to record the amount of the transaction ("payment/debit," "fee," or "deposit/credit"), and a final column for a balance. Notice how each entry is made, keeping a running balance. (Don't forget to subtract the ATM withdrawals as they are made!) If you write a check, write the check number, the date, the recipient, and the amount in the check register. If you deposit funds or withdraw cash from the ATM, write the amounts down in the register. If you record all your transactions, keeping the running balance becomes much easier. At the end of the month, you will only need to figure in per-check charges, the service charge, and interest.

Keeping it Safe

Many bankers offer one, simple, commonsense piece of advice for the neophyte bank customer: **Keep track of your ATM card and checkbook.**

Your ATM card can be an incredible convenience—and at times it can be a real life-saver. But it is also the single most dangerous card in your wallet. When you receive the card, you also receive a Personal Identification Number, or PIN. Some banks allow you to select your own combination of four numbers; others randomly assign the number to you. It's the PIN that tells the ATM who you are. After you insert the card into the ATM, you'll be asked to enter your "secret code number"; that's your PIN. It takes both, your PIN and your card, to get into your account. *Don't* keep the PIN with your ATM card.

Let's assume that you've selected your PIN, 0814. Here's what *not* to do:

1. Don't write your PIN on a Post-It and stick it to your ATM card.
2. Don't write your PIN down on a piece of paper and keep it in your wallet or purse.

The reason for these rules is simple. If you lose your wallet or purse, whoever finds it also finds your PIN. Then he or she can walk over to the nearest ATM and proceed to clean you out. At most banks, your liability is only $50, but why run even this risk? Memorize your PIN and destroy the paper it's written on. That's the best advice. If you are somewhat absent-minded, write it down and then hide the number somewhere safe—NOT in your wallet or purse!

Now assume your PIN, 0814, is your birthday. (You chose it because you know you can remember it.) Frankly, that's almost as dumb as keeping your PIN attached to your card. If someone lifts your wallet or purse, he also has your ATM card—and the first number he'll try will be your birthdate, which he can easily find on your driver's license. Consider using one of your parents' birthdates instead.

Also, be careful when you use the ATM machine. If someone is crowding you in an effort to see what your PIN is, just walk away from the machine. And take a look around before making a transaction, especially at night. Don't let yourself become a target! One of the more popular crimes at night is a quick mugging after someone's gotten cash from the ATM.

Never lend the ATM card to a friend.

If you lose your ATM card, or your checkbook, inform the bank immediately. Reporting a loss immediately will protect you from losses above $50.

Last Thoughts

Get to know your bank representatives. The new accounts rep, the tellers, even the branch manager. Don't be afraid to ask to meet the bank manager during your first visit. You might not think you're important enough or that you're depositing enough money to warrant her attention, but do it anyway. It will place you head and shoulders above most other students who are opening accounts. Also, if the manager knows you, she may be more willing to waive some of the bank's rules. In other words, she might be in a position to do you a favor just when you need it.

Safeguard your checks and the ATM card. You wouldn't leave money sitting around; don't leave these items around either.

Finally, just because you have a checking account, it doesn't mean that every merchant in town will honor or accept your check. Other pieces of identification may be required—a major credit card for instance. If you don't have one, he may not accept the check.

Don't throw a fit; be polite. Try to get to know the merchants you'll be dealing with regularly. If the merchant knows you, he'll be more willing to take a chance on you. You know he's not really taking a chance, but how is *he* to know? This is the real world. In the real world, there walk bad-check artists, forgers, thieves, and scamsters. Your cherubic smile and youthful good looks offer no protection to a businessman.

Your checking account will perhaps be your first, and certainly your most enduring, real-world experience. Make the best of it.

GIMME SHELTER

▼ ▼ ▼

For years Stuart fantasized about what it would be like to have his own place . . . and no one to answer to. Despite his best efforts to block out the "noise" at home, the messages still got through.

"Are you eating at home, dear?"

"I know you want to go out, but couldn't you please babysit your sister?"

"Turn off the stereo! It's driving me crazy!"

"Clean your room! It looks like a pigsty in there!"

"Other people need to use the phone, you know."

"Have a good time, dear, but be sure you're home by midnight."

When he moved into his place, things were going to be different! And they were.

Stuart had trouble with his two roommates. Neither of them could be counted on to kick in for the utility bills. He ignored the bills, pushing them aside until after the big party he had been planning. This was going to be a party that no one was going to forget.

It was the night the music died. And the lights went off. And the air conditioner stopped running. It was the night the utility company shut off the power to Stuart's apartment.

And to this day, Stuart and his friends remember that party.

Freedom! You've dreamed about it, planned for it, fantasized about it—and now it's actually going to happen! Your own place. No more parental curfews. No more endless arguments about mealtimes, music, and mess. Yes, these parental hassles will disappear when you make the move to live on your own. But there's a trade-off. Having your own place also means no more free maid service, free rent, or free utilities, and no more cooked meals, stocked refrigerators, or ever-flowing fountains of spending money when you run short. All these "perks" of living at home now become your responsibilities.

What's more, these are only a few of the responsibilities you'll face when you rent or lease your first apartment. Here are some of the questions you'll be asking yourself: Who will my roommate be? How will I get to school? Can I find an apartment close to shopping and campus? Whom do I call if I have problems with my roommate? and What happens if something breaks?

The answers to these questions will vary for individual situations, but for the new college student there is the proverbial good news and bad news. The good news is that the services provided by most college or university housing offices far exceed anything you'll ever encounter again—it'll never be easier to make an informed decision on where to live. The bad news is that finding—and keeping—a place of your own isn't always fun or easy.

The Housing Office: Two Examples

Upon being accepted by the college or university of your choice, you'll more than likely receive some information concerning housing from the school. Let's look at a couple of housing-office operations to see what they offer.

Becky White has a tough job. As Manager of Community Living of the Department of Housing & Dining for the University of California at Berkeley, she helps thousands of students find housing. The university and affiliated housing accommodates approximately 10,000 of Berkeley's 30,000 students, leaving two-thirds of the students to find housing in the community, where housing stock is scarce. And expensive. Students and their parents often suffer sticker shock when they learn of the high rents paid for apartments in buildings that are sometimes 40 to 50 years old. Students compete in the rental market as well as in the classroom and on the playing fields. Becky therefore suggests that students planning to attend Berkeley for the fall semester begin their housing search in May!

Like many housing managers, Becky White beats the bushes for rental listings. She often speaks to various local boards of realtors asking for their assistance in providing listings of rentals for Berkeley students. She also calls apartment-house owners and property managers in search of adequate housing. At Berkeley, hundreds of listings are made available. The listings are computerized and are updated daily. But these listings are exclusively for students. Becky reminds students to bring a student ID or acceptance letter to gain entry to the housing office.

But Berkeley's campus housing office provides services that go beyond just listing places available for rental. Counselors are available to help students select the right situation based on their needs. These counselors are able to put some students in touch with others looking for housing. And the assistance doesn't end when the student walks out of the campus housing office and into the new apartment. Housing office counselors often act as combination mediators/arbitrators/go-betweens and convenient shoulders-to-cry-on when problems arise. Becky White, for example, has interceded for students with their landlords and has helped settle roommate squabbles.

Let's head south. San Diego State University (SDSU) also has a very active housing office. When there is a tight housing market, SDSU sponsors an intensive four-day workshop in July dealing with off-campus housing. SEARCH (Student Education and Research Concerning Housing) helps you find not only an apartment but often a roommate as well. The SEARCH workshop features a panel of · experts including Martha Vickers, SDSU's Off-Campus Housing Coordinator. Martha also invites an attorney and a property manager to sit on the panel. Panel members answer students' housing questions. And since many students don't even know what kind of questions to ask concerning housing, SEARCH provides the questions as well. At SDSU the Housing and Residential Life Office publishes and distributes a housing guide called the *Aztec Housing Guide*. This guide provides an overview of over 100 apartment houses. Rent prices, security deposits, type of term available (lease term or month-to-month), and amenities are noted for each apartment complex. Additionally, this guide uses student polls to rate the apartments in such areas as social atmosphere, recreational facilities, pest control, manager relations, and neighborhood safety. Maps show the location of the apartment complex in relation to the campus.

It's comforting to know you're not alone in your search for shelter. Campus housing offices like those at Berkeley and SDSU are willing and able to help.

Desperately Seeking Shelter

Here are some housing tips to remember when you begin your home-hunting mission.

CALL EARLY Students who get in touch with the housing office early have the best selection. This is especially critical for large schools in an urban environment such as New York City and the Cambridge/Boston area.

KNOW THE RULES There may be some restrictions or requirements you need to know about. For instance, at some colleges, first-year students are not allowed to live off campus. Or you may need a student ID or acceptance letter to use the housing services. Check ahead.

USE THE LISTINGS The type of information available on each listing varies from school to school. Most students seem to focus on a few key features: the type of dwelling (house , apartment, condo, room in a private home), the address, and the price.

SET YOUR OWN PRIORITIES The information taken for the listings is generally the result of a 3-to-5 minute telephone call from a property manager. Overloaded housing offices cannot customize lists for each student. You have to build your own list using your own criteria. For example, you may build a list using these factors: rent, number of bedrooms, location relative to the campus, and amenities.

USE THE FOLLOW-UP SERVICES Counselors are available for more than helping you select the right situation based on your needs, budget, and lifestyle. Don't forget the "mediation" counseling when things get too weird with your new roomie or your landlord begins acting like Freddy Krueger.

SEEK PARENTAL GUIDANCE Help is allowed and encouraged. If your folks can give you any assistance, take it!

ATTEND WORKSHOPS If your school offers a housing workshop, like SDSU's SEARCH program, sign up and attend.

Preparing to find a place to live may take more time than you imagined. However, addressing these issues and needs before looking at apartments will save you time: you'll be looking at only those apartments likely to be right for you.

Beginning the Search and Seizure Mission

When you walk out of the housing office with a stack of listings and a map, you'll be ready to begin the search.

To start, you'll probably meet with a property manager—or superintendent—who'll show you an apartment or two. The property manager often lives in one of the units, and is usually available during business hours and for any emergencies. When you're shown what's available for rental, you should have a list of questions ready. You obviously know the location and you probably know the rent that's being asked for the apartment, but there's some other stuff you need to know.

▼ *Is the apartment available on a month-to-month rental or will a lease be required?* (A lease is a formal agreement between tenant and landlord; it guarantees that the tenant may stay for a specified period of time at a fixed rent.)

There are advantages and disadvantages to both types of rental agreement. Many apartment complexes catering to students will offer a school-year lease, usually 10 months. Others may require a 6- or 12-month lease. (Becky White reports that many apartments in the Berkeley area require a 12-month lease. In that case students who go home—or elsewhere—for the summer are forced to pay rent on a empty apartment during the long break.) Leases can offer *security*. For example, if you sign a 10-month lease for a two-bedroom apartment at $325 per month, you are protected from any increases in the rent and are assured of a place to stay. The landlord is also happy because the unit is continuously occupied and provides a steady cash flow. But leases can be hard to break. If you don't like your neighbors, or their dog, you may be stuck with them for the duration.

The advantage of a month-to-month rental is *flexibility*. If the place isn't all it's cracked up to be, or you're having trouble with your roomie, you can give 30 days' notice to the manager and you are free to leave. However, the reverse is true as well. The landlord can ask you to leave after giving you 30 days' notice. And the landlord can also raise the rent.

Generally, you won't be able to choose between month-to-month or leasing. Each apartment complex has a standard operating procedure. However, this issue might be a critical factor for you in deciding where to live.

▼ *Is the apartment furnished or unfurnished?*

Again, there are advantages and disadvantages. Furnished apartments tend to be more expensive. But having a furnished place means you can dispel the image of leaving for college driving a U-Haul and towing your car. Unfurnished apartments are cheaper. But you'll still need something to sleep on besides your sleeping bag, and boxes don't usually make it for the long haul as dressers or tables. So you'll have the expense of buying furniture, or the trouble of begging and borrowing it from friends and relatives. Many students rent furniture; you might be surprised at how reasonable this option is.

▼ *What utilities or appliances come with the apartment?*

Most apartments come equipped with a stove and a refrigerator. But you should ask about these appliances anyway. And if you're interested in air-conditioning, garbage disposals, dishwashers—any special utility or appliance—ask about them as well.

▼ *What are the average costs of utilities for the apartment?*

Ask the property manager to give you a rough estimate of what you can expect to pay for gas and electricity in your apartment. Ask about the rates *and* the amount. Although the rates a local utility will charge won't vary within a single service area, the actual amount you pay can vary significantly under different conditions. If, for example, you want air-conditioning, you can expect to pay more for electricity. An all-electric apartment may sound great, but in most places electric rates are more expensive than natural gas or heating oil.

▼ *What amenities are offered?*

Does your apartment complex have a pool, a recreation area, a laundry room, a weight room, air-conditioning, adequate parking/assigned parking, elevators, balconies, cable? Do you really *want* those things? What do you want? Need? What can you afford?

▼ *How secure and safe is the apartment complex?*

Do the doors leading into the complex require keys? Is the parking lot well-lit? Are the hallways? Are there smoke detectors or burglar alarms? Does your apartment door have a deadbolt? Can all your windows be locked? Is there a doorman on duty at all times? Is there a security patrol or Neighborhood Watch in the area?

▼ *What are the other tenants like?*

If you're going to be the only student in a complex of senior citizens, life can be miserable for all concerned. Landlords of apartment complexes that rent to students normally have a good idea of the percentage of their total tenant population that students represent. There is no hard and fast percentage that makes one complex better than another. It just makes sense that you'll feel more comfortable in a apartment house where you'll fit in socially.

▼ *What deposits will be required?*

Most apartment complexes require a *security deposit* as well as the first month's rent before you can move in. A security deposit is money you pay to the landlord for assurance that you'll fulfill all the obligations of your rental agreement. Let's go back to our two-bedroom apartment at $325 a month. If the landlord requires a security deposit of $250 and the first month's rent, you'll need $575. (A cashier's check, money order, or cash will probably be stipulated, although a personal check may be accepted.) Why is a deposit required? The security deposit may be used to remedy any default in the payment of rent. Or it may be used to pay for cleaning after you vacate or for repairs above and beyond normal wear and tear. For example, the landlord may charge you to clean the carpet and deduct this sum from your security deposit, but you can't be charged for the cost of replacing the carpet unless you've destroyed it. How? If you cut two-foot squares out of the carpet to make mats for your VW, you're likely to be held liable for the damage. Simply, the security deposit is protection for the landlord.

Here's some not-so-great news. You might also be asked for a deposit which includes the *last* month's rent. Continuing our example, this would mean a total deposit of $325 + $325 + $250 = $900. But if you pay last month's rent at the beginning, you won't have to pay rent for the month following your giving 30 days' notice.

NOTE: Make it a point to find out what you have to do to be eligible for a full refund of your security deposit. It just may be worth your while to clean the carpet yourself if that means you'll get all the money back. Also find out if you'll receive interest on your security deposit—some states require landlords to pay interest on any funds they're holding simply against possible damage or cleaning costs.

Now let's take stock of our apartment hunting. This two-bedroom place looks very attractive. The rent is reasonable, and the apartment complex is close to campus. The other tenants are mostly students. There's a small pool, a laundry room with washers and dryers, and a large recreation room with pool and ping-pong tables. Your unit has only one assigned parking spot, but you and your roommate can rent another for an additional $15 a month. The apartment's unfurnished, but it does have a refrigerator, stove, and dishwasher. There's only one bath, but it has a nice shower and tub. The apartment complex is secure. Utilities are reasonable. Best of all, there's a small balcony that overlooks the common area and the pool. No pets are allowed. It's the best place yet.

You've made up your mind . . . .

You'll Take It!

Once you and the landlord come to terms, you'll be asked to fill out an application. Some of the information requested on the application form may seem personal— that is, none of "their" business. But fill it out, completely. Name, current address, Social Security number, date of birth, driver's license number, and current telephone number are all fairly standard. The application may also ask for additional information, such as present occupation, previous employment, current income, name of bank with account numbers for savings and checking, a list of creditors, and a list of personal references. Information like this helps the manager determine your reliability.

But the application may include other, not-so-obvious questions. "What is the model and make of your car?" "What is your mother's maiden name?" "Whom do we call in case of emergencies?" Here's why. The manager needs to know which car is yours for security reasons—to ensure that no uninvited guest is parking in your assigned space. And your mother's maiden name is something only you would know, so it's just an additional form of positive identification. And, in an emergency, the manager may want to be able to contact a friend or relative.

> **NOTE:** There may also be inappropriate questions, which you are not required to answer. Nor should you. Questions concerning sex, race, or religion are considered discriminatory, an invasion of privacy, and illegal. If you are asked such questions on the application—or verbally—let the campus office know.

The property manager may then run a credit check on you, just as a bank would. Property managers don't want tenants who don't pay their rent or bills.

Now comes the *rental agreement*—a contract between you, the tenant, and "them," the landlord or a designated agent. Contracts are binding legal documents. Important stuff. Somewhere on this document there will be a place for your signature. Once you've signed your name, you've agreed to everything printed and written on this document. Read it. *All* of it. You'll be surprised how thorough these documents are—how they seem to cover every possibility. Rental agreements, which are fairly standard now, have developed this thoroughness through a process of trial and error. (Speaking of trials, rental-agreement contracts also hold up in court.)

Let's take a look at a sample rental agreement found on pages 23 to 24. In most cases, the rental agreement will identify the landlord and tenant—the "Parties"—and specify the exact apartment—the "Property"—to be rented. It may also include a listing of specific furniture, appliances, and services. The term of the agreement (month-to-month or lease period) will be stated, as well as the amount of rent and when it's due. Who is responsible for the utilities is also covered. The agreement will also cover restrictions on

Rental Agreement

National Housing and Economic Development Law Project Form Lease (California)

1. Parties

The parties to this Agreement are _____
_____,
hereinafter called "Landlord," and _____
_____,
hereinafter called "Tenant." If Landlord is the agent of the owner of said property, the owner's name and address is
_____
_____,

2. Property

Landlord hereby lets the following property to Tenant for the term of this Agreement: (a) the property located at _____
and (b) the following furniture and appliances on said property: _____
_____
_____

3. Term

This Agreement shall run month-to-month, beginning on _____

4. Rent

The monthly rental for said property shall be $_____, due and payable on the first day of each month.

5. Utilities

Utilities shall be paid by the party indicated on the following chart:

	Landlord	Tenant
Electricity	_____	_____
Gas	_____	_____
Water	_____	_____
Garbage collection	_____	_____
Trash removal	_____	_____
Other	_____	_____

6. Use of Property

Tenant shall use the property only for residential purposes, except for incidental use in his trade or business (such as telephone solicitation of sales orders or arts and craft created for profit), so long as such incidental use does not violate local zoning laws or affect Landlord's ability to obtain fire or liability insurance.

7. Tenant's Duty to Maintain Premises

Tenant shall keep the dwelling unit in a clean and sanitary condition and shall otherwise comply with all state and local laws requiring tenants to maintain rented premises. If damage to the dwelling unit (other than normal wear and tear) is caused by acts or neglect of Tenant or others occupying the premises with his permission, Tenant may repair such damage at his own expense. Upon Tenant's failure to make such repairs, after reasonable notice by Landlord, Landlord may cause such repairs to be made and Tenant shall be liable to Landlord for any reasonable expense thereby incurred by Landlord.

8. Alterations

No substantial alteration, addition, or improvement shall be made by Tenant in or to the dwelling unit without the prior consent of Landlord in writing. Such consent shall not be unreasonably withheld, but may be conditioned upon Tenant's agreeing to restore the dwelling unit to its prior condition upon moving out.

9. Noise

Tenant agrees not to allow on his premises any excessive noise or other activity which disturbs the peace and quiet of other tenants in the building. Landlord agrees to prevent other tenants and other persons in the building or common areas from similarly disturbing Tenant's peace and quiet.

10. Inspection by Landlord

Unless Tenant has moved out, Landlord or his agent may enter the dwelling unit only for the following purposes: to deal with an emergency (such as fire); to make necessary or agreed repairs, decorations, alterations or improvements; to supply necessary or agreed services; or to show the unit to prospective or actual purchasers, mortgagees, tenants, workers, or contractors. Unless there is an emergency, Landlord must give at least 24 hours prior written notice of his intent to enter and the date, time, and purpose of the intended entry. (In case of an emergency entry, Landlord shall, within 2 days thereafter, notify Tenant in writing of the date, time, and purpose of the entry.) Tenant shall have the right to refuse to allow any entry (except for an emergency) before 9 AM or after 5 PM. If Tenant objects to an intended entry between 9 AM and 5 PM, Landlord shall (where feasible) attempt to arrange a more convenient time for Tenant. Landlord's entries shall not be so frequent as to seriously disturb Tenant's peaceful enjoyment of the premises and shall not be used to harass Tenant.

11. Security Deposit

a) Upon signing this Agreement, Tenant shall deposit with Landlord the sum of $_____ as a security deposit. This deposit (with any interest accrued under the subparagraph (c) of this paragraph) may be applied by Landlord toward reimbursement for any costs reasonably necessary to repair any damage to the premises caused by Tenant, to clean the premises (where Tenant has not left the premises as clean as he found them), or for due and unpaid rent.

b) Landlord shall inspect the premises within one week prior to Tenant's vacating the premises and, before Tenant vacates, shall give Tenant a written statement of needed repairs and the estimate cost thereof.

c) Within two weeks after Tenant vacates the premises, Landlord shall return to Tenant the security deposit together with interest of one-half of one per cent for each month Landlord held the deposit, less any deductions Landlord is entitled to make under subparagraph (a) of this paragraph. If Landlord makes any such deductions, he shall, within two weeks after Tenant vacates the premises, give Tenant a written itemized statement of such deductions and explanations thereof.

12. Landlord's Obligation to Repair and Maintain Premises

a) Landlord shall maintain the building and grounds appurtenant to the dwelling unit in a decent, safe, and sanitary condition, and shall comply with all state and local laws, regulations, and ordinances concerning the condition of dwelling units.

b) Landlord shall take reasonable measures to maintain security on the premises and the building and grounds appurtenant thereto to protect Tenant and other occupants and guests of the premises from burglary, robbery, and other crimes. Tenant agrees to use reasonable care in utilizing such security measures.

c) If repairs are now needed to comply with this paragraph, Landlord specifically agrees to complete the following repairs by the following dates:

Repair   *Date*

_____ | _____
_____ | _____
_____ | _____
_____ | _____

d) If Landlord substantially fails to comply with any duty imposed by this paragraph, Tenant's duty to pay rent shall abate until such failure is remedied. This subparagraph shall apply to defects within Tenant's dwelling unit only if Tenant has notified Landlord or his agent of such defects. The remedy provided by this subparagraph shall not preclude Tenant from invoking any other remedy provided by law to Tenant for Landlord's violation of this Agreement.

13. Subleasing

Tenant shall not assign this Agreement or sublet the dwelling unit without the written consent of Landlord. Such consent shall not be withheld without good reason relating to the prospective tenant's ability to comply with the provisions of this Agreement. This paragraph shall not prevent Tenant from accommodating guests for reasonable periods.

14. Failure to Pay Rent

If Tenant is unable to pay rent when due, but on or before such due date he gives Landlord or his agent written notice that he is unable to pay said rent on time and the reasons therefore, Landlord shall attempt to work out with Tenant a procedure for paying such rent as soon as possible. If, after 10 days, Landlord and Tenant are unable to work out such a procedure, Landlord may serve a notice to pay rent or vacate within 3 days, as provided by California Code of Civil Procedure Section 1161.

15. Destruction of Premises

If the premises become partially or totally destroyed during the term of this Agreement, either party may thereupon terminate this Agreement upon reasonable notice.

16. Notice of Termination

Tenant may terminate this Agreement upon 30 days' written notice thereof to Landlord. Landlord may terminate or change the terms of this Agreement upon 60 days' written notice thereof to Tenant unless the property is located in an area covered by "just cause" for eviction regulations, in which case those regulations control. No notice shall be valid, however, if the Landlord's dominant purpose in serving it is to retaliate against the Tenant because of Tenant's attempt to exercise or assert his rights under this Agreement or any law of the State of California, its governmental subdivisions, of the United States, or because of any other lawful act of Tenant. Any such notice shall contain a statement of the reasons for termination or change of terms, and if such statement be controverted, Landlord shall have the burden of proving its truth. This paragraph shall not affect Landlord's right to terminate for cause after expiration of a 3-day notice given pursuant to California Code of Civil Procedure Section 1161.

17. Termination and Cleaning

Upon termination of this Agreement, Tenant shall vacate the premises, remove all personal property belonging to him, and leave the premises as clean as he found them (normal wear and tear excepted). If the property is located in an area covered by "just cause" for eviction regulations, Landlord must comply with these regulations in order to terminate or evict.

18. Lawsuits

If either party commences a lawsuit against the other to enforce any provision of this Agreement, the successful party shall be awarded court costs from the other. Landlord specifically waives any right to recover treble or other punitive damages pursuant to California Code of Civil Procedure Section 1174.

19. Notices

All notices and rent provided by this Agreement shall be in writing and shall be given to the other party as follows:

To the Tenant: at the premises.

To the Landlord: at _____.

WHEREFORE We, the undersigned, do hereby execute and agree to this Lease.

LANDLORDS: TENANTS:

_____   _____
(signature)   (signature)

        _____   _____
        (date of signature)   (date of signature)

_____   _____
(signature)   (signature)

        _____   _____
        (date of signature)   (date of signature)

use of the property. For example, it might specify that the apartment may be used only for "residential purposes." This means you can only live in the apartment—not use it as a place of business. The agreement will state that you have an obligation to "maintain the premises." This means you have to keep the place reasonably clean and you should try not to wreck anything. Conditions and times for inspections by the landlord may be spelled out. The amount of the security deposit and its applications will be included. Finally, the rental agreement will specify what obligations the landlord has to repair and maintain the property, what happens when the rent is not paid in a timely manner, and what the procedures are for terminating the agreement.

NOTE: It may be possible to add to, or subtract from, the rental agreement before you sign it. For instance, if the landlord has agreed to put in new locks on the door, ask to have this written in.

Are you getting the idea that this whole apartment thing is fairly businesslike? You're right. It is. When you rent an apartment in a businesslike manner, you'll find that the whole procedure goes smoothly. No surprises.

Read the rental agreement. Don't push it away with an "It's all Greek to me!" comment. Ask questions and be sure you understand the answers. The managers of apartment complexes are there to provide the answers to first-time renters. They expect the questions.

You've selected the apartment, filled out an application, signed a rental agreement, and handed over the required first month's rent plus security deposit. The place is yours for 10 months. But don't breathe a sigh of relief just quite yet. There's a lot more to do.

Getting Turned On

Most apartment complexes won't charge for water or garbage collection. But you'll usually be required to pay for electric, gas, telephone, and cable services.

The housing office or the property manager can provide the telephone numbers of the public utility companies. You have to call in advance to arrange for service. Expect to pay a "hook-up" charge. A local gas and electric company may charge anywhere from $5 to $30, depending on the kind of service provided to your unit. As a new customer, you might also be asked to pay a "meter-deposit," which is usually two times the average monthly bill. This deposit is refundable and is applied as a credit to future billings.

Telephone service may be a bit complicated, since you won't necessarily be able to handle all your telephone needs by dealing with a single company. The local operating company will provide you with the lines and service, but not the telephone itself. You must either lease or purchase a telephone. And you'll pay to be hooked up.

Let's look at an example. Pacific Telephone's average charge for connecting service is $34.75, plus $3.00 for a touch tone. But here's the good news: the charge can usually be spread, interest-free, over your first three bills. And there are no additional charges for new customers.

The type of local telephone service you select varies. When you call to arrange for service, a customer service representative will go over all the available plans and charges. For example, you may have a choice between the "Unlimited Plan" and the "Measured Plan." The Unlimited Plan, for $8.35 a month, lets you make as many local calls as you like and includes the monthly service fee. The Measured Plan, at $4.45, provides the basic service, but each call is counted, timed, and billed. The actual prices for the service you buy may vary, but the idea is the same. You make your choice based on how (and how much) you'll use your telephone. (*Hint:* One customer service service rep said that she wouldn't recommend a Measured Plan to college students, because they tend to make a lot of calls.)

There's one other decision for you to make: selecting a long-distance provider. You've seen the commercials, so you probably know who these providers are, and you've probably decided already which provider will meet your needs. Or you can make a decision by inaction. If you don't make a choice, the local tele-phone company will randomly assign you a long-distance phone company.

If you can't live without MTV or ESPN, then you'll have to call the local cable company. Again, charges vary by the level of service you want. Premium stations such as HBO, Showtime, or Cinemax will cost more than the basic cable package.

When you're finally hooked up to all these lifelines, you'll also find out how expensive maintaining an apartment can be. It's not just the rent payment.

As a student on a budget, you'll learn all sorts of ways to cut your utility bills. You won't need to keep the thermostat on "ROAST" all night during the winter; and you won't need to keep the air-conditioner on "ARCTIC" during the hot months. You'll find that telephone calls, especially long-distance calls, made outside of peak hours (9:00 AM to 5:00 PM, Monday through Friday) will be cheaper. These are acquired, but easily acquired, skills.

It may appear that all that remains is to move in your "stuff," but there is one more item you must attend to prior to taking occu-pancy. Inspection.

Inspector Clouseau

Inspections conjure up specters of military precision, cleanliness, and order. In the old war movies, some eagle-eyed sergeant is always dragging his white gloves over every nook and cranny in some poor private's barracks. Everything has to be just so.

That sergeant should be your role model when you inspect your new apartment. Most apartment complexes will have inspec-tion and inventory forms like the one shown on page 28. These forms should be completed before you move in. (This same form may reappear when you vacate the apartment.) They usually include lists that are very comprehensive and should leave some room for brief notes. As you inspect the apartment with the property manager or landlord, make certain that the list notes any discrepancies

Inventory and Inspection Form

Both the manager or owner and tenant(s) are expected to sign and receive an executed copy of this statement: 1) within 3 days of taking possession of the premises and 2) at the End-of-Term Inspection upon termination of the tenancy.

Beginning Inventory Date _____ Signature of Tenant _____ Signature of Manager/Owner _____

End-of-Term Inspection Date _____ Signature of Tenant _____ Signature of Manager/Owner _____

The apartment covered by this agreement is # _____ located at _____ , California.
(address)   (city)

NOTE: This inventory list is for your protection. Be sure to indicate the condition of each item. Note the number of items where applicable and location and nature of all soil and damage, etc. Be specific and check carefully. Additional comments may be attached.

Area or Furnishings	Condition Upon Arrival	Condition Upon Departure (note deterioration beyond reasonable use and wear)	Est. Cost of Restoration (Incl. labor & materials)
KITCHEN			
Cupboards			
Floor Covering			
Walls, Ceiling, Counter Surfaces			
Stove & Oven (pans, grills, etc.)			
Refrigerator (trays, butter dish)			
Sink & Garbage Disposal			
Tables & Chairs			
Windows (coverings, screens, etc.)			
Other (please specify)			
LIVING ROOM			
Floor Covering			
Walls & Ceiling			
Tables & Chairs			
Sofa			
Windows (coverings, screens, etc.)			
Other (please specify)			
BATHROOM	#1 #2	#1 #2	
Floor Covering			
Walls, Ceiling, Tile			
Shower			
Tub			
Sink & Medicine Cabinet			
Toilet			
Windows (coverings, screens, etc.)			
Other (please specify)			
BEDROOM			
Floor Covering			
Walls & Ceiling			
Desk & Chairs			
Dresser			
Bed (frame, mattress, box spring)			
Closet (doors & tracks)			
Book Shelves			
Windows (coverings & screens, etc.)			
Other (please specify)			
ADDITIONAL ITEMS			
Air Conditioner			
Heater			
Thermostat			
Closets			
Doors (locks, etc.)			
Electric Fixtures, Outlets, Lamps			
Other (please specify)			Total: $

Release of Security Deposit

Check **one** of the following:

( ) On _____ , the manager/owner inspected the premises with tenant and found them to be in satisfactory condition, wherefore the manager/owner agrees to refund the sum of $ _____ , the FULL amount of the security deposit.

( ) On _____ , the manager/owner inspected the premises with tenant and found them to be in need of cleaning, replacement or repair, beyond reasonable use and wear. The estimated costs of repair, replacement, cleaning or other tenant's default under the lease, is $ _____ and will be deducted from the security deposit. Both the manager/owner and tenant agree that the unused portion of the deposit shall be refunded to the tenant. At the same time the refund is made, the manager/owner will furnish the tenant with a statement accounting for any deductions, including a detailed itemization of labor and materials.

NOTE: Any refund of a deposit must be returned to the tenant(s) within two weeks after the date of this agreement as provided for under California Civil Code 1950.5.

Date _____

Signature of Manager of Owner _____

Signature of Tenant _____

Address to Mail Deposit: _____

between what should be there and isn't, and what shouldn't be there but is. Chipped tile around the sink, a shelf missing from the refrigerator, a towel bar broken in the bath, cracked linoleum in the kitchen, missing switchplates, or any item that is in disrepair or in poor condition should make the list.

Even if everything looks fine, take a few extra seconds to make sure that everything works. Turn on the faucets and the lights. Light the burners on the stove, and check the oven. Flush the toilets. See if the refrigerator compartment is cool. Open and close the windows, and check the locks. Make sure the showerhead works. Do the heating and the air-conditioning units work? Of course, it isn't practical to try everything. For example, you may later find an electrical outlet that has no power. If you do, inform the property manager as soon as possible. Remember, the landlord is responsible for repair and maintenance of your apartment.

The reason for all this thoroughness? You don't want to be blamed—and held financially liable—for damage you didn't do.

Movin' In

Most moving days for students are fairly low-key. Usually you'll be moving in with just a few boxes of books and necessities, and some suitcases. More than likely, your definition of "household goods" is what you're able to fit into the car. In this case, you can do it yourself. However, if you've managed to accumulate more "stuff," you graduate to the next level of moving in. This level includes having a few friends help you move in, provided there are some larger, heavier objects. These items arrive via a rented U-Haul truck or trailer, or if you're lucky, maybe a friend's van or pickup. Payment for these friends might be pizza on the floor of your new place.

But perhaps you'll be arriving in style, with plenty to move. Furniture, stereo and video equipment, closetfuls of clothes, books—the whole enchilada. This means professional movers, and when you hire them, be prepared to pay top dollar. Professional movers offer a variety of services, and each service provided costs you money. The movers can arrange to pack your belongings, including wrapping breakables, boxing up books, and placing your clothes in wardrobe boxes. This service is delivered at an hourly rate, and you'll be charged for the packing material as well. Then you'll pay for the move itself. The distance that the goods are transported, the weight of those goods, and any storage required will determine that cost. Finally, you can have the movers unpack all your items as they're unloaded . . . again, at an hourly rate.

When selecting a moving company, ask friends and neighbors who have recently moved about their experiences. If they recommend the company that moved them, then give that firm a call. The moving company will send a representative to your place to make an estimate. But don't stop there. It's a good idea to get two or three estimates for comparison purposes. Rates will vary, but usually not by much, because many of the charges are standard and these companies are very competitive. But by comparing a couple of companies, you can get a good idea of what the standards are . . . and you can take advantage of any special services that might be offered.

If you're only moving a short distance, you might consider hiring a small, local firm. The rates of local movers are usually lower than those of the bigger, interstate companies. These firms are not insured—or bonded—in the same fashion as the big firms are. However, these companies are frequently very efficient—just what you need for a short haul.

If you do hire professional interstate movers, your household goods will be covered by the firm's insurance. The driver of the moving van will check your belongings when they are loaded and he will point out any damage before the goods go on the truck. Check your belongings when they arrive and note any damage. If any items are damaged, you'll be able to file a claim.

NOTE: You can choose to pack your own goods, to save money. In fact, you can often buy the packing material from the moving company. However, if you do, and goods packed in those boxes are damaged on delivery, the moving company is not liable.

Living in Junior's Room

Boarding is not extinct. If you don't want the hassle of worrying about furnishing an entire apartment, or being concerned with utilities, then boarding may be an option. Many people in college towns rent rooms to students. "Empty nesters"—parents whose kids have already left home—may let you have Junior's old room for a reasonable price. In this unique rental arrangement, you are actually renting a room in someone's house, so you get all the benefits of living at home. But the rules you left behind at home may well be traded for a different set.

Berkeley's Becky White comments that the majority of the problems she deals with after finding housing for a student are disputes between room renters and their "landlords." Sometimes a new landlord doesn't understand a renter's rights. "On more than one occasion," she says, "a student has returned to find all his belongings packed in a box and left in the front yard." Disturbing? Yes! Also illegal. But not always easy to handle. If a student finds himself in this situation, it is certainly the time to bring in the campus housing counselor to mediate the problem.

Let's say you've chosen to live in Junior's old room. Junior is now an associate at some law firm in Atlanta, and mom and dad have decided to rent his room. Maybe they miss the pitter-patter of little collegiate feet clomping through their halls, or maybe they're looking to bring in a few more dollars in their retirement. Whatever. Just keep in mind that you are living in *their* home. So, instead of worrying about utilities and amenities, you have a new list of concerns. These concerns should be addressed before renting the room.

To clarify these concerns, you can sign a room-rental agreement like the sample on page 32. Use the agreement to specify all the rules you'll have to follow and all the privileges you expect to enjoy. As you can see, a rental agreement covers several points on which you and your landlord should agree.

PRIVACY This is the big issue—and the biggest difference between renting an apartment and boarding in a private home. You

ROOM RENTAL AGREEMENT

This is an agreement between _____(landlord)
and_____(tenant)
for the rental of a room located at _____
_____.

This agreement shall run from month-to-month, beginning on _____.
It may be terminated by either party giving to the other a written 30 day notice.
Rent is due in advance on the_____day of every month, in the amount of
$_____.
Tenant has paid a deposit of $_____which is fully refundable within
fourteen days following termination of tenancy. As provided in California Civil Code
1950.5 deductions for unpaid rent, damages caused by the tenant beyond normal wear
and tear, or reasonable cleaning costs, may be made, if necessary, with an itemized list
of these costs given to the tenant.

Utilities shall be paid by the landlord, or shared in the following manner:
_____.

The tenant and landlord agree to abide by the following:

Room Maintenance: The tenant shall keep room in a clean, sanitary condition.

Privacy: The landlord may enter the room only after giving 24 hours advance notice, or
after obtaining the tenant's consent, or in an emergency.

Kitchen Use:_____

House Privileges:(i.e. use of laundry, TV, phone, etc)_____

_____

Guest Policy:_____

Quiet Hours:_____

Music:_____

Parking:_____

Pets:_____

Other:_____

SIGNATURES

_____   _____

should expect and receive privacy. That room is yours; you've rented it, and the landlord must give you 24 hours' notice before entering, unless there is an emergency. (Dust on the night table does not constitute an emergency.) But privacy is a two-way street. You are entitled to your privacy, and so is the family you're living with.

UTILITIES In most cases, utilities (gas, electricity, and so forth) will be paid by the landlord. But if you want something special—say, your own air-conditioner—you may be asked to pay for your share.

TERM It's a good idea to rent rooms on a month-to-month basis. That way, either you or the landlord can end the arrangement by giving 30 days' notice.

You may also use the agreement to come to an understanding regarding the following concerns:

KITCHEN USE Do you get to whip up some of your own favorite meals? Can you use the microwave or other appliances? Are meals included in the rent? Are you expected to eat with the family?

HOUSE PRIVILEGES Can you use the laundry facilities? television? telephone? pool? hot tub? If so, when and under what conditions?

GUEST POLICY Can you have friends over? Overnight guests? Can your sister stay in your room when she's visiting?

Here are some other issues that should be addressed before you rent a room. How does the landlord feel about your playing the stereo? Can you park in the driveway or the garage? Can you fix or wash your car on the premises? Are there quiet hours? How will your landlords treat your coming and going at odd hours—either for classes or returning late from studying or a job?

Try to cover all the possibilities with your landlord. If you come to a clear understanding with your potential landlord, you stand a good chance of having a successful experience. Some students have found boarding to be an ideal living situation and heartily endorse renting a room in a house. But everyone agrees that boarding presents different problems and challenges than renting an apartment.

Roommate, Roommate, Wherefore Art Thou, Roommate?

If you plan to have a roommate, now's the time to think about it. If you make a mistake and select the wrong roomie, financial woes could be right around the corner. Let's face it; your roomie is half the rent! After spending hours looking for a place, months deciding on what college to attend, and years completing the requirements to make it to college, shouldn't you spend a few minutes investigating the person you are going to live with?

Martha Vickers is SDSU's roommate guru. She moderates the SEARCH workshop, and she has also done her fair share of moderating disagreements between roommates. At the workshop, she distributes a sheet with 27 questions to help students in selecting a roommate. Take a look at these questions (page 35). Sure, it sounds like you're playing a game of "Scruples" or paging through The Book of Questions, but the answers are important to your mental, and ultimately, financial, well-being. And just knowing the questions can help you focus on the perfect roommate for you.

The four-day workshop allows students to get to know one another. Where did you grow up? What is your major? Why did you pick this school? Were you involved in sports or extracurricular activities? Will you be working while going to school? Do you consider yourself to be conservative, liberal, or middle of the road? What music do you like? Are you a morning person or a night person?

This is also a good time to find out how much your prospective roomie can afford to pay for rent. Some other questions might include: Does she have a car? Would she prefer a condo, an apartment, or a house? What kind of furniture will she be bringing? Does she have a stereo, TV, microwave? What's important in the apartment complex itself: security? pool? recreational facilities?

QUESTIONS FOR THE ROOMMATE SELECTION WORKSHOP

Getting Acquainted

1. Tell us your name, hometown, major, and class standing. If you are a freshman, where did you go to high school? If you are a transfer or graduate student, where did you attend college previously?
2. Why did you pick this university?
3. How did you arrive at the SEARCH program — drive, ride with someone else, or fly?
4. Tell us something interesting about yourself.
5. What do you like to do in your spare time?
6. Do you consider yourself to be conservative, liberal, or middle-of-the-road?
7. Do you consider yourself to be a religious person?

Housing Needs

1. How much is the most you could afford to pay for rent?
2. Do you plan on sharing a bedroom, or do you want your own bedroom?
3. Do you have a car? Are you able to live away from the immediate campus area?
4. Are you looking for an apartment, condo, house, or room in a private residence?
5. Are you looking for a furnished or unfurnished place? What kind of furniture (including TV and stereo) are you planning to bring?
6. Does it make any difference whether you sign a lease or a month-to-month rental agreement?
7. What kind of conveniences do you want — dishwasher, air-conditioning, security building, jacuzzi, recreational facilities, etc.?

The Perfect Roommate

1. What kind of music do you like?
2. What hours do you like to sleep? study? socialize?
3. What do "clean" and "messy" mean to you?
4. Do you smoke? Do you care if your roommate smokes cigarettes? pipe? cigars?
5. What are your attitudes toward alcohol, marijuana, and/or other drugs?
6. Would you object to your roommate's having overnight guests? of the opposite sex?
7. Would you like for your roommate to share cooking and grocery shopping with you?
8. What is your attitude toward pets?
9. On a scale of 1 to 10 — with 1 being very quiet and studious and 10 being a wild partier — where would you rank yourself?
10. List 3 of your personal habits that a roommate might find annoying.
11. List 3 "pet peeves" you have about other people's behavior.
12. What is your source of income?

And then you can ask questions that can *really* help in deciding who that perfect roommate is. What kind of music do you listen to? What hours do you like to sleep? study? socialize? Do you
smoke? What are your feelings about drugs and alcohol? What
about overnight guests? What is your source of income?

If you like classical and she likes jazz, if you wear furs and
she's a card-carrying member of Greenpeace, if he's offense and
you're defense, things might not be starting out on the right foot.
Yes, life may be a bit more stimulating, and you both might grow
intellectually. However, the reality of it is that you'll probably end
up hating each other's guts.

You must also decide if you're going to rent or lease the
apartment as *cotenants* or if you intend to rent alone and have a
subtenant. If you and your roommate are cotenants, you are
both responsible to the landlord. If you have a subtenant, you
are responsible to the landlord . . . and your roommate is responsible to you. There are risks and rewards in both agreements. If
you choose to have a subtenant, however, you can agree to
some controls over your situation. You may, for instance, agree
that either one of you can end your arrangement on thirty-days'
notice. If you've made a bad decision selecting a roommate, an
agreement like this can be very attractive. Or, you may want the
same security that the landlord enjoys—you might have your
subtenant sign a lease. Now if things get rocky, you might have
to grin and bear it.

Martha Vickers recommends a roommate agreement like the
one SDSU provides to its students (see page 37). This is a contract
between roommates that sets the rules for sharing an apartment.
The thinking is, if you've already agreed to a host of contingencies
in writing, life will be smoother. This roommate agreement makes
sense; by listing possible issues, you are actually resolving them
before you and your roommate encounter them. The splitting of
expenses, the sharing of cooking and cleaning responsibilities, the
use of personal property, and a guest policy should all be
addressed before they become issues. A good agreement even has
a clause for how unforeseen conflicts can be resolved.

Roommate Agreement

This is a legally binding agreement. It is intended to promote household harmony by clarifying the expectations and responsibilities of all residents. Each person should receive a copy of this agreement.

This agreement is in effect for the duration of the tenancy entered into on _____, 19_____,

for the property at _____

_____

TENANTS who have signed a contract with the owner/agent are:

_____

_____

They are considered principal tenants.

SUBTENANTS (all occupants of the premises not on contract) are:

_____

☐ This contract is for a **month-to-month tenancy** which may be terminated by any party with a 30-day written notice to owner and roommates
   OR
☐ This contract is for a **fixed-term lease** beginning on _____ and ending on _____. Any departing roommate will continue to be responsible for the rent until a replacement, who is acceptable to the owner/agent and the remaining roommates, is found.

DEPOSIT has been paid in the amount of $_____, shared by the roommates as follows: _____

Each roommate will receive his/her portion from the landlord at the end of the tenancy, or when a replacement roommate moves in and pays a deposit to replace the departing roommate's portion. Each roommate is responsible for charges associated with the damages he/she or his/her guests caused. Each person is expected to do appropriate cleaning upon termination to avoid deductions.

RENT totals $_____ per month, payable on the _____ day of the month, and shared by the

roommates as follows: _____

Amounts do not have to be equal.

UTILITIES shall be shared in the following manner:

ITEM	ACCOUNT IN NAME OF	AMOUNT OF DEPOSIT	DEPOSIT PAID BY (name)	HOW BILL SHARED	ROOMMATE RESPONSIBLE TO PAY
Electricity/Gas					
Phone—local*					
Phone—long dist.*					
Cable Television					
Water					
Other (e.g. newspaper) specify:					

*All unclaimed telephone charges shall be divided equally among

HOUSEHOLD SUPPLIES including paper goods and cleaning materials will be purchased and cost divided equally by all roommates.

KITCHEN USE

☐ Food expenses shall be shared evenly by all roommates. Preparation of meals shall be determined by an attached schedule which can be flexible.
   OR
☐ Food is to be bought by each roommate. There is to be no borrowing of food without prior approval. A separate space will be designated for each person's groceries.

Each roommate agrees to do his/her own dishes promptly after use and empty the trash as needed.

CLEANING

All roommates agree to share the responsibilities of cleaning and maintenance of the premises. This includes vacuuming, dusting, mopping, cleaning bathrooms, cleaning kitchen (refrigerator, oven, burners, floors), cleaning windows, woodwork, light fixtures, doing yardwork if applicable.

☐ Each roommate takes responsibility for the following portion of chores: _____

   OR
☐ A schedule is attached showing rotation of cleaning duties.

PERSONAL PROPERTY

The following items are contributed for use by all members of the household _____

All roommates agree to refrain from borrowing any other items without prior approval of the owner.

GUEST POLICY

Roommates have discussed and agree to these guest rules:

# of days per week guest OK _____, between hours of _____

overnight guests _____, guests for meals _____

parties _____

CONFLICT RESOLUTION

Each housemate will try to develop mutual cooperation and clear communication with all others. Continuing disputes will be resolved by:

☐ Decision by household consensus   ☐ Majority vote

☐ Decision by principal tenant   ☐ Decision by landlord

☐ Mediation (SDSU Housing Advisor or Community Mediation Program)

ADDITIONAL AGREEMENTS (keys, quiet hours, music/TV, parking, pets, use of alcohol, drugs, tobacco, etc.)

_____

_____

SIGNATURES OF ROOMMATES

_____   _____

_____   _____

Movin' Out

Hey, it's been a great year! Your two-bedroom apartment within walking distance to the campus has turned out to be a terrific place. In fact, you're thinking about renting an apartment there for next year. Your roommate has been ideal. His bedroom occasionally looks like a disaster area, but the kitchen, living room, and bath have always looked presentable. Now all that remains is the long-awaited summer vacation.

But wait. Make sure your euphoria about summer doesn't dull your brain. Remember, you must give 30 days' notice, in writing. This doesn't have to be a document worthy of the Magna Carta. A simple, signed note will do.

And, remember inspections? You're now a private. Get the cleaning supplies out and make the place ready for inspection. You are actually working for money. That money is your security deposit, handed over almost a year ago. If the apartment is clean, undamaged—or at least its condition is the same as it was when you rented it—you can expect to get the lion's share of your deposit back. Leave the place a mess and you accomplish two distasteful feats at once. First, you are willfully throwing away money. Second, you help establish a reputation that can follow you around a small campus community, and make it hard for you to rent another place next year.

There's a lot to this freedom stuff, isn't there?

A CAR IN
EVERY GARAGE

▼ ▼ ▼

I once owned a Dodge American. It was, in today's vernacular, a "pre-owned" automobile. In truth, it was a used car—a very used car. It wasn't pretty, but the price was right, $150; and it looked like it'd get me from my apartment to work.

From the very first day I drove it, this car was a mystery. It overheated whenever it was driven at speeds over 50 miles per hour and I was forever pulling off the freeway in search of a service station. It seemed that every time I stopped, I'd fill the radiator with water and dump at least two quarts of oil into the crankcase. But I don't recall ever putting gas in the tank. Was this the first steam-powered vehicle on California roads?

Of all the cars I have owned, this Dodge American had the most personality. But "Old Less Than Faithful" was truly a disaster waiting to happen. I never test-drove the old Dodge on the freeway, so I didn't know about its aversion to speed . . . which it had. I didn't bother to see if it leaked oil when I parked it . . . which it did. I didn't take it to a mechanic to determine if any major repairs were imminent . . . which they were. In short, I never bothered to do the things that today I would call prudent. I bought this dream car on a whim, and within days, it was becoming a nightmare. I paid $150 for a set of wheels, and that's just what I got—a set of wheels.

It finally blew up as I was crossing the San Francisco-Oakland Bay Bridge.

Realizing my error, I sold the car to a Navy chief for $75. His teenaged son drove the car to school for two years—never on the highway.

Except for a few urban pockets where mass transit can still provide service to nearly every commuter, cars have become a necessity of life. Unless you're attending a city college or university, more than likely you'll need a car.

When you're young and free, the temptation is great to buy on impulse. The big lesson here is to avoid impulse-buying. For the most part, cars can't be returned. And the true costs begin *after* you've made the purchase.

What are the ongoing, everyday costs associated with owning a car? What will the monthly payments be? Is there a way to estimate maintenance costs and other incidentals? In short, can you afford a car?

Odd as it may seem, sociologists point out that no other purchase will reflect what you think of yourself—and what others think of you—as much as a car purchase. Cars have come to reflect success, wealth, personality, and availability. In general, status. Let's face it. Heads turn when a Porsche 911 cruises by. No one looks twice to see who is driving the four-door sedan.

What Price Auto?

"The average person puts the cart before the horse," says Alan Vaks, a 20-year veteran in auto sales. "Many times, a first-time buyer decides he's ready to buy a car and heads to the dealership. He spends a couple of hours test-driving and then negotiating for the car of his dreams. It's not until he's gotten himself completely revved up for this hot car and he's ready to sign the purchase contract, that it hits him—he just doesn't have enough money to drive his 'dream' home. It's a big disappointment, one he could've easily avoided if he'd just thought some things out before he came to us."

How do you avoid this disappointment? By asking yourself some practical questions and being honest with the answers. These questions—which have to do with affordability and financing—are:

1. How much of a down payment can I afford?
2. How much in monthly payments can I afford?
3. What will my insurance costs be?
4. How much will maintenance cost?
5. What other incidental costs should I be taking into account?
6. If I don't pay cash for the car, do I qualify for financing?
7. How do I compare loans?

It's easy to see why the affordability and financing of your car are critical. "Affordability" means you're able to pay for the car, either all at once, or on a monthly payment plan. "Financing" is what you do when you have to borrow money—from your parents, credit union, bank, finance company, and so forth. These should be the foremost issues you address. A closer look at these costs will help you determine if you're ready to buy a car, and, if you are, how much you'll be able to spend.

Let 's assume you can't pay cash for the car. You have to shop for a loan. You may actually borrow the money from your parents and pay them each month, on whatever terms you agree upon. (Keep in mind, however, that loans from parents come with certain strings attached, like, "How can you afford to head to Fort

Lauderdale for spring break when you owe us money?") Or you may secure a loan from a traditional lender: credit unions, banks, thrifts or savings & loans, or automobile financing arms such as Ford Motor Credit (FMC) and General Motors Acceptance Corporation (GMAC).

Down Payment

The first order of business is the *down payment*. This is the initial amount of money you pay upfront for the purchase. Obviously, the bigger the down payment, the less that remains to be financed. Most traditional lenders will be flexible with regard to the amount of the down payment, but the rule of thumb is the bigger the better! To encourage you to make a larger down payment, lending institutions may offer more favorable loan rates as incentives. For example, one credit union offers an 11.00% loan for 48 months on a new car when a 20% down payment is made. That same credit union offers 11.25% when a 10% down payment is made, and 11.50% when there is no down payment.

Of course, even if there's not a reduction in the interest rate charged, a larger down payment reduces the monthly payment, saving you money over the life of the loan. If you borrow less, there's less to pay back.

Let's say, for instance, you've selected a car that costs $3,500. It's a used car, so the loan rates will be slightly higher than they are for a new car. When you go to your friendly credit union, you're told you'll be charged 11.75% for any 48-month loan, regardless of its size.

If you're strapped for cash, you may decide to put $500 down on the car and finance the remaining $3,000 with the credit union. When the loan officer calculates the monthly payments, you find that you'll be paying $78.63 a month for 48 months. This means you'll pay a total of $3,774.24 in the course of the four years.

But suppose you're not strapped for cash. You've worked all summer and have a big enough pile to make a $1,500 down payment. Then, at 11.75% your monthly payments on a 48-month $2,000 loan would be $52.42. Over four years you will pay $2,516.16.

Now notice the difference between the cost of the two loans. The finance charges on the $3,000 loan come to

$$\$3,774.24 - \$3,000 = \$774.24$$

while the finance charges on the $2,000 loan are

$$\$2,516.16 - \$2,000 = \$516.15.$$

Subtracting the finance charges of the smaller loan from the larger one, you come out $258.08 ahead.

It's up to you to decide the size of your down payment on the basis of what you can afford to spend now, and how much you can afford to spend as time goes by. If you have the cash, it's a good idea to make a sizable down payment. But, practically, you may not be able to do that.

Monthly Payments

Now, let's determine the purchase price of a car based on an affordable monthly payment. Let's say that, after considering your budget, you decide you can afford a $100 monthly car payment and you have $2,000 ready for a down payment. The question now becomes "How much car can you buy for your $100 a month loan payment?" You can go around to dealers and ask that very question—or you can calculate the payment yourself by finding out the going interest rate, then using the table on page 44.

Let's say you've called some banks and your credit union, and the best loan available is 12% for 48 months. Now use the table. To calculate your monthly payment, cross 12% and 48 months and you see that for every $1,000 borrowed, your monthly payment will be $26.33. Borrowing $4,000, or four times that amount, will result in a monthly payment of $26.33 X 4 = $105.32. This is very close to what you had in mind. Add the $4,000 loan to the $2,000 down payment and you see that you can afford a car that costs $6,000. (A more precise way to figure out your affordable price is to divide $100 by the 26.33 factor from the table. The result is 3.797. Multiply that number by $1,000 and you get a loan of $3,797, which results in a $100 monthly payment.)

INTEREST RATE PAYMENT TABLE

	Payment per $1,000		
Interest Rate	48 months	60 months	84 months
10.00%	25.36	21.25	16.60
10.25%	25.48	21.37	16.73
10.50%	25.60	21.49	16.86
10.75%	25.72	21.62	16.99
11.00%	25.85	21.74	17.12
11.25%	25.97	21.87	17.25
11.50%	26.09	21.99	17.39
11.75%	26.21	22.12	17.52
12.00%	26.33	22.24	17.65
12.25%	26.46	22.37	17.79
12.50%	26.58	22.50	17.92
12.75%	26.70	22.63	18.06
13.00%	26.83	22.75	18.19
13.25%	26.95	22.88	18.33
13.50%	27.08	23.01	18.46
13.75%	27.20	23.14	18.60
14.00%	27.33	23.27	18.74
14.25%	27.45	23.40	18.88
14.50%	27.58	23.53	19.02
14.75%	27.70	23.66	19.16
15.00%	27.83	23.79	19.30

Insurance

Next, you'll need to determine what your insurance costs will be. This is hard to do in advance, but there are some factors you should be aware of. Most insurance companies consider you young and dangerous. Good students may pay less, but invariably "he" pays more than "she." Some of you will be covered under your parents' plan, but you may be paying that cost as well. For "guesstimation" purposes, let's say that insurance will run $45 a month; it may be substantially less or astronomically higher. (In some cases, monthly insurance costs exceed the loan payment!)

Maintenance

Maintenance costs are almost impossible to figure in general terms because the factors in the equation will vary with the type and age of the car. For example, parts for foreign cars, like a Volkswagen Jetta, are affected by the rate of currency exchange. The classic Mustang you own may require classic prices on replacement parts. Furthermore, older cars need tune-ups more frequently than do today's computerized cars. And some new developments have raised prices but lowered costs. For example, new alloys in spark plugs have lengthened their lifetime by a factor of four! You might pay a little more, but they'll last a lot longer.

While many costs are simply unpredictable, it's important to get some guesstimates for the particular car you have in mind. Talk with the previous owner if you're buying a used car from a private seller. She may have all her repair and maintenance records. A quick check of these records will give you an excellent estimate of the annual expenditures you may expect. If you are buying a new car, ask the salesperson. The salesperson should be versed in the maintenance requirements and costs for the models he is selling. You can also talk with a mechanic who is familiar with servicing the type of car that you're considering. Finally, you can do some research. *Consumer Reports* publishes maintenance histories and costs on a fairly frequent basis. A thorough check of some or all of these sources can often make the difference between your owning a car or the car's owning you.

Meanwhile, for the purpose of our illustration, let's say that you have determined that your car will cost you $400 in annual maintenance. This figure breaks down to about $33 a month. Is this the end of the costs? Almost.

Incidentals

Incidentals include registration, license plates, parking fees, gasoline, window washer solvent, Armor-All, washing . . . . You get the idea. These are the pernicious little costs that you never seem to think about when you're picturing yourself behind the wheel of the dream machine. For example, many universities require students to purchase parking passes, which allow you to park on campus. Or if you're sharing an apartment in an apartment complex that allotted only one space for your unit, you might have to pay a fee to park your car on the premises. For our illustration, let's guess that incidentals will come to about $30 a month.

Qualifying for a Loan

If you don't pay cash for the car, will you qualify for a loan? Remember your checking-account experience! Before you can get a loan, the banker will make a determination of your creditworthiness and your ability to pay. For our example, let's say that you have a part-time job paying $100 a week. The bank, or credit union, may then accept you as a suitable credit risk. Or, the loan officer can ask your parents to co-sign the loan. This means that if you default on the loan—that is, you stop making payments—the loan becomes the responsibility of mom and dad. But you don't want it to come to that if you can help it. Buying, financing, and subsequently paying off a car can be one of the best ways to establish credit.

Comparing Loans

Now, about that loan. It pays to comparison-shop. Calling ahead to get interest-rate quotes will save you time. While you're shopping, keep in mind factors other than the interest rate when determining which loan is right for you. And you'll have lots of choices. For example, some new car loans are made for 84 months—seven years! Some loans preclude pre-payment; that is, you actually would have to pay a penalty for paying your loan off early. Some institutions might require that you take out loan insurance. This ensures that if you die, the loan will be satisfied. (Not that you would care one way or the other, but this is a common feature . . . and it adds to your cost.) But when you're making your choices, you need to remember one inescapable truth: the longer you pay, the more you pay. Go back to the table on page 44. If you finance $3,000 at 12% for 48 months, you will pay a total of $3,791.52 to the lending institution. That includes $791.52 in interest charges. The same loan amount at the same rate for 60 months means that you pay $4,003.20 over the life of the loan—that's $1,003.20 in interest costs!

Monthly Total

Let's summarize. You've found the car of your dreams at a cost of $4,500. You have $1,500 for the down payment and will be financing $3,000 at 12% for 48 months, which gives you a monthly payment of $78.99.

Line up the other costs and let's see what we have:

```
Monthly payment.......................................$ 78.99
Insurance................................................$ 45.00
Maintenance (estimate)............................$ 33.00
Parking..................................................$ 15.00
Incidentals...............................................$ 30.00

TOTAL MONTHLY EXPENDITURE...........$201.99
```

So, your college chariot will cost you over $200 a month to own and maintain! In our example, you were working part-time and earning $400 a month. Half your income will be going to keeping you in wheels.

The Art of the Deal

The key to buying a used car is to determine costs today and down the road. When you're making a deal, three criteria are essential: mileage, price, and mechanical condition.

Mileage

The average car racks up 12,000 to 15,000 miles per year. Less is good, more is bad. An adjunct to mileage is the age of the car. A car that's seven years or older with average mileage (84,000 to 105,000) is considered a high-risk buy. And the combination of mileage plus age tends to have a bad effect on parts. New tires, for instance, should be considered at anywhere between 20,000 to 50,000 miles, depending on the size of the car and how it is driven. At 50,000 miles, you might need to replace valves. The frequency of tune-ups varies with the make and model, but any engine or transmission lasting beyond the 100,000-mile mark is considered a gift. You might think that you have a sweet deal for a seven-year-old car with 90,000 miles on it for only $1,000. However, if you put $2,000 or more into the car two months later, replacing tires, valves, and shocks, then the deal wasn't so sweet after all.

DEALING AND WHEELING

Not all cars are purchased off a dealer's lot. Many first-time car buyers purchase their cars from a private seller. Here's an example of a student who used the resources of the blue book to sell her car and "trade up" to a fancier model.

Suzanne decided to sell her Mazda 323. She dutifully took it to three auto dealers.

"I was surprised to see how close each of the offers came to one another," she reported. "They were all within $200. I then decided to try to sell my car by advertising in the newspaper at a price halfway between what I was offered and the price the dealers were selling my car for on the used-car lot. This arrangement enabled me to make another $700 . . . and I also saved the buyer about that much."

Now Suzanne had to find herself a new set of wheels. She picked out the car she wanted, another Mazda. But this time it was a sportier RX7, and she was buying the car from a friend. She called various dealers and checked to see if they had a comparable car on the lot.

"I know I didn't 'steal' this car from my friend," she said, "but I was paying less than what the dealer would have charged. My friend also got a better price from me than a dealer would have given her."

Of course, if you find a seven-year-old car with 40,000 miles on it which was owned by the proverbial little old lady from Pasadena, it could be a great find.

Price

Price is subjective once the car is driven. As soon as a car is driven off the lot, the price is purely perception. Auto dealers, buyers, and private sellers often use the "blue book" as a guide for price. Actually, there are *several* blue books. Keep in mind that libraries, leasing companies, and dealers, all of whom have a version of this price reference book, may be quoting from different sources. While the blue book is only a guide, it will help you determine a price that is fair to you as well as the seller.

Let's say someone trades in, or sells, his car to a dealer. The wholesale blue book price is $3,000. Depending on the car's condition, inside and out, the dealer may offer the seller any price between $2,400 and $3,300. The dealer then turns around and offers the car for sale at $4,800. Joe College walks in to buy the car. If Joe buys the car for $3,800, assuming it meets his criteria, it's probably a fair deal. If Joe ends up paying $4,700, he just hasn't bargained enough.

Before buying a car, become familiar with the blue book price and know the range between what a dealer will pay for the car and what he will price it on the lot to sell. This is part of the negotiation process. Once you know the high-to-low range, you'll feel more comfortable with your purchase if the price you pay is somewhere in the middle of the spread.

Shop around and know the market. Not only do you get educated in the process, but you negotiate from a position of knowledge. You often get a better price. And you'll also feel more confident in the purchase you've just made.

Mechanical Condition

The final, and perhaps most important, criterion is the actual working condition of the car. If you're not an expert in the field of auto

TIPS FROM A PRO

"If you do buy a used car, you're better off going to a new-car dealer rather than to a used-car lot," says Alan Vaks. His rationale is that when a new-car dealer takes in used cars, usually as trade-ins, he frequently keeps only the best of these cars and wholesales the rest. Where do these wholesaled cars resurface for sale? You've got it, at used-car lots.

In today's market, a used car priced at or over $5,000 tends to be a better quality car. But keep in mind that the profit margin on used cars is greater than that on new cars. Vaks suggests that you negotiate. "Let's say that a dealer paid the previous owner $2,700 for his car. He puts $350 in improvements into the car and then factors in another $300 commission for the saleswoman reselling it. The dealership's cost is $3,350. This car will be placed on the lot for $5,200—but a dealer would probably accept $4,200 if he's anxious to move the vehicle." Even at that price, the dealer clears $850, a 25% return. New cars generally have a 10% mark-up, giving you less room to negotiate and making it harder for the dealer to compromise on price and still show a profit.

Vaks also points to some other advantages to buying a used car from a reputable new-car dealer. The car has probably been inspected, prepared ("prepped"), and repaired for resale. Best of all, most dealers offer a 30-day warranty on major parts to ensure against unexpected problems.

One final note on used-car warranties. What happens if the car you purchased has a major problem on the 31st day, or shortly after the warranty expires? Does the buyer have any recourse? According to Alan Vaks, "If the dealer cares about his reputation, he'll work something out. But he's not going to volunteer to cooperate. Be persistent and work your way up the chain of command. Start with the salesperson who sold you the car, then the sales manager, then the general manager, and if necessary, the owner. Your best strategy is to be polite and refuse to take no for an answer."

mechanics, don't pretend to be. Bring along someone who is, or rely on the expertise of a knowledgeable mechanic. If you are purchasing the car from a private seller, ask the seller if she would be willing to have it taken to a mechanic for inspection. (Dealerships may also allow an independent inspection. Ask for it, even if the car comes with a short-term warranty.) This visit to the mechanic could either give you tremendous peace of mind, or save you hundreds, possibly thousands, of dollars. Inexpensive computer diagnostic equipment can test for a variety of problems. Mechanics can also inspect alignment, brakes, transmission, shock absorbers, battery, and so forth. Naturally, no one can guarantee a car's total performance, but a skilled mechanic can uncover an obvious sign of trouble you might overlook.

> **CAUTION:** From a private seller you won't receive a warranty or a guarantee that the car won't give you problems. Most private sellers want either cash or a cashier's check. (They're concerned that a personal check might bounce and you'd get a "free" car.) If the car blows up as you're making a U-turn in front of the seller's house, that's just your tough luck. When you buy from a private seller, you buy "as-is." That's why experts recommend that you have the car examined by a reputable mechanic.

Maintain an Even Strain

Now that you own a car, it's a good idea to learn a little about maintaining it. After all, this is not a pair of jeans you just bought, but a complicated, expensive, mechanically sophisticated piece of equipment.

Putting gasoline in your car is not maintenance, it's sustenance. Maintenance includes checking the oil, water, brake fluid, and transmission fluid levels. It also means keeping your tires properly inflated. If you're not a "hands-on" type of driver, frequent a full-service station. At these stations the attendants will ask if they can check these items. When someone asks, "Check your oil, sir?" answer "Yes!"

Most mechanics consider self-service gasoline stations to be the bane of routine maintenance. "If you use a self-service station," cautions one mechanic, "you have to make some checks yourself.

When a warning light comes on, it's generally too late. Some damage has already been done."

After buying your car, the first order of business should be a thorough reading of the owner's manual and the maintenance manual. (Sometimes these are separate books, and sometimes this information is combined in one book.) If your manuals are missing and you have a fairly recent model year, order the books from a local dealership. These manuals don't just outline a schedule for routine maintenance; they are also helpful in learning how to operate your new car.

Routine checks of simple fluid levels could save big money and make operating the car much safer. Manual in hand, locate the dipsticks for your fluids—oil, brakes, and transmission. Then, follow instructions. Generally, oil should be checked twice a month and adding oil is a relatively simple matter. However, it's important to know the difference between the radiator and the crankcase when you do this simple task. Oil in the radiator or water in the crankcase leads to disastrous problems. The radiator should also be checked, but only when the engine is cool. Remove the radiator cap. If you don't see any fluid, add water or antifreeze. The label on the container of antifreeze gives you a primer on radiator maintenance. Finally, most cars now have a reservoir for window-washing solvent. If it's low, refill it.

You should also change the oil and replace the oil filter on a periodic basis. The owner's manual will recommend the frequency. Most mechanics urge you to change the oil and replace the filter either at least twice a year, or every 6,000 miles. These are among the easiest of the routine maintenance jobs and almost anyone can master the few steps.

Don't neglect your tires. Check them twice a month as well. You can purchase an inexpensive, accurate pressure gauge for a couple of bucks and check your own tires. Keep them inflated at the recommended pressure, which is written right on the tires. Again, the owner's manual will be helpful here. Why is checking the tires important? Underinflated tires wear out faster and you will also have poorer gas efficiency. Depending on the size of the car, the type of driving you do, and the normal road conditions, tires can wear out anywhere from 20,000 to 70,000 miles.

But there's a bit more to maintaining a car than merely checking fluid levels and checking tire pressure. Other common maintenance items include:

TUNE-UPS Tune-ups usually include changing spark plugs, checking and adjusting the timing, changing the air filter, and checking the transmission. Newer cars require major tune-ups at 30,000 to 50,000 miles, while older models may require tune-ups every 15,000 miles.

BRAKES Have brakes checked whenever you bring your car in for routine maintenance. *Note:* A two-footed driver will wear out his brakes more quickly because he puts constant, though slight, pressure on the brakes.

SHOCK ABSORBERS Push your car down at the fenders; if it bounces, you need new shocks. If you find your car leaning to one side, you probably need new shocks.

FRONT-WHEEL ALIGNMENT While on a straight section of road, release your steering wheel for a short time. If the car "pulls" to one side or the other, have the alignment checked. You can destroy new tires with as little as a few thousand miles of driving with a poorly aligned car. (P.S. Don't do this test during rush hour.)

BATTERY Have the battery checked whenever you take the car in for maintenance.

Movin' Up

You may already own a car. But if you're thinking about moving up in class for college, you should consider a few other items. Remember Suzanne and her Mazda 323 to Mazda RX7 upgrade? There were some costs Suzanne didn't figure on when she bought her sports car. First, her insurance rates were raised by $400 a year. She had to switch from regular unleaded to premium unleaded gasoline, a big increase in the price per gallon, which was exacerbated by the fact that she also gets poorer gas mileage with the RX7. If Suzanne blew a tire with the 323, it would cost her about $60 to have it replaced. But high-performance, extra-wide steel-belted radials for the RX7 could set her back about $200 each! The incidentals can add up very quickly with a new purchase.

CHAAAARGE!

▼ ▼ ▼

Steve was getting ready for the Senior Prom. As a university fresh-
man, he knew that he would be one of the few "college men" at the
prom. He wanted to make a big impression. Last year he had been
a high school senior, just another faceless guy in the high school
crowd. Now it was his night to be Big Man on Campus, the return-
ing collegian. Preparing for his date, he rented a limousine the
size of an ocean liner, selected the most expensive tuxedo, brought
two elaborate corsages to his date's house (one for the mother—he
thought that was a nice touch), and had his hair razor-cut. To pay
for all this, Steve got special pleasure out of using his new credit
card. He charged each and every purchase. After all, a BMOC
doesn't carry cash.

Dinner was at a very trendy, very upscale restaurant with prices to match. Steve spared no expense from appetizer to dessert. As the evening wore on, Steve knew he'd really impressed his date . . . and many other prom-night couples.

That was, until the maitre d' discreetly called Steve away from the table to tell him that there was "a little problem" with his credit card. His charges had exceeded the limit. Returning to the table, a redfaced Steve muttered something about "a terrible mistake," and asked his date if she might pay for dinner. He promised that he'd repay her on Monday. Steve saw the entire evening crumble before his eyes. His dream night had been built on a house of cards—credit cards. Steve had wanted his date to be speechless, awed by the spectacular evening. She was "speechless" all right: she didn't utter a single word for the rest of the evening.

A major credit card—Visa, MasterCard, American Express—can be a valuable tool for a student. Having a credit card means you can buy things even if you're short of cash. Unexpectedly large purchases—like a semester's worth of books—can be paid for with a credit card. Sometimes when a merchant won't accept a check, a credit card can come to the rescue. Credit cards also come in handy during an emergency. When your car breaks down on your way home for the holidays, you can use your credit card to pay for repairs. And a major credit card can serve as your first means of establishing credit.

However, excessive use of credit cards can be dangerous to financial health. While you may be able to purchase something now that you don't have ready cash for, you must pay the bill eventually. And you'll pay it with finance charges that can run as high as 20%+! So it's important to think of your credit card as just another tool in your financial toolbox. Use it when you have to, when you need to, and sometimes when you want to, but don't use it excessively or exclusively.

But before you get a credit card, you need some answers. How do you get a credit card? Is one credit card better than another? Can you get a credit card even if you don't have a job? What happens if you lose your card or someone steals it? What exactly are finance charges? The answers to these, and other, questions can help you get your credit card and use it wisely.

Free Money?

▼ *Just what is a credit card anyway?*

Obviously the piece of plastic with your name on it is the card, but the term "credit" often confuses people. In essence, credit is a loan. In this case, think of credit as *time*—time allowed for payment for anything sold on trust.

▼ *What's an issuer?*

Typically, banks, credit unions, savings & loans, department stores, and now, even telephone companies, issue, or offer credit cards. The credit card issuer is lending you money, and trusts you to pay it back. The credit limit of your card—$300, $500, or $1,000—is determined by the issuer.

▼ *How does a credit card work?*

Let's walk through a credit-card transaction and see what happens. You're at a department store and find a sweater that you just have to buy. Better yet, it's on sale! You pull out your credit card and pay for the sweater, $21.88. You now have a sweater and the merchant has a signed credit card slip. That signed slip represents payment. The merchant processes the charge, either electronically or on paper. If the merchant is directly tied to his bank by electronic means, authorization for the purchase is almost instantaneous and the credit to the merchant is posted overnight. He receives his payment the next day. A paper trail takes a bit longer. A merchant will hand-carry his receipts to his bank, where they are processed and then credited to the merchant's account.

NOTE: Credit-card issuers receive a fee from merchants for any transaction, usually 1 to 5%. (That's how the credit-card issuer makes its money—a small fee on a high dollar volume.)

▼ *When do you have to pay the money back?*

At the end of the billing period, you receive a bill that itemizes your credit-card purchases. If you made your purchase early in the billing cycle, it could be nearly a month before you actually pay for your sweater. This time delay is known as "float."

Where Do I Sign?

College campuses are awash in credit-card applications. The student center, campus bookstore, cafeteria, and dorms are just a few of the places you may find an application for that piece of plastic.

The questions on the application range from asking for your name, address, and Social Security number to inquiries about your employment history, your checking and savings accounts, and other credit cards you might hold. Other questions include how long you've lived at your current residence, income, outstanding debts, and if you own a car.

Although the questions are straightforward, credit approval is not automatic. Each credit-card issuer establishes requirements that must be met before a card is issued. Minimum requirements for getting a credit card will vary from issuer to issuer. For example, to apply for a credit card from Citibank, the banking arm of New York–based Citicorp, you must be registered as a full-time student at a four-year college or university. (Citibank is currently testing programs for community colleges.)

But if you're applying for a MasterCard or Visa card through Bank of America, you have to meet some additional requirements. U.S. citizenship is a requirement. And it's not enough to be a checking-account customer—you must further demonstrate that you have been a *good* customer for six months. (What's a good customer? One who doesn't bounce checks.) Additionally, you must show a monthly income of at least $200.

Meeting the minimum requirements is no guarantee that your application will be approved. "Credit is not easy to get. It's one thing to complete an application, and it's another to be approved," says William Ahearn, Vice President of Public Affairs at Citibank. "Well over half the applicants are turned down." This is because a credit-card issuer must use your application as a starting point to evaluate you as a credit risk. Take Citibank, for instance. How does Citibank evaluate an application? Citibank uses a scoring system that helps weed out the good from the bad credit risks. "This system gives us what we feel is our competitive edge," adds Ahearn. "Citibank uses a scoring model with a number of different criteria. We ask the student applicants some questions and then compare the answers to those that were given by current cardholders. A 'good' applicant's score would reflect characteristics similar to good customers we already have. For example, cardholders with larger savings balances usually have better credit performances than those with low or no balance. An applicant with a checking account would score higher than another applicant without one. Applications are approved from the perfect score to a range that's somewhere in the middle."

What *are* these criteria. Like the formula for Coca-Cola or the ingredients for Kentucky Fried Chicken, these are highly guarded secrets. But all credit-card issuers have their criteria and use them to make credit-risk estimations.

If you qualify for a card, it means that you have met the issuer's criteria—and that the issuer will trust you to charge purchases up to a certain amount. This amount is your *credit limit,* which is usually $300 to $500 for a first-time card holder. (You may also see, on your first monthly statement, a charge for the annual fee. These fees vary, but typically range between $20 and $50.)

If you don't qualify, don't panic. Apply to another major credit-card issuer. The requirements for this issuer may be different from those of the issuer you applied to first. Another option is to apply for a retailer's credit card. Almost all retailers, such as Sears, Marshall Fields, Nordstrom's, Neiman Marcus, and Macy's, issue their own credit cards. The retailers also use criteria to judge your creditworthiness and ability to pay, but these are often easier to meet than those of major credit-card issuers. If you do secure a retailer's credit card, you can use it to build a credit history over a fairly short period of time—say, four to six months. Then you can apply for a major credit card again.

What's the single most important factor that determines whether or not you get a credit card? Your credit history. Remember that you must show up to the issuer with a clean credit report. And the issuer finds out about your credit history from TRW. So let's look at TRW and see how this company may affect your ability to get credit.

The Credit Bureau of Investigation

TRW Credit Data Systems, also known as TRW, is a clearinghouse of credit information used by many subscribers to determine the credit-worthiness of individuals. When you apply for a credit card, or other forms of credit such as a car loan or home mortgage, the grantor of the credit will usually check out your credit history with TRW. In fact, when you submit an application to the issuer of any kind of loan, you are giving that issuer permission to check you out with TRW.

"Credit Data Systems maintains a library of credit history information," explains Michael Van Buskirk of TRW's Information Systems & Services operation. "It's a get-and-give situation, with credit grantors both contributing to and using payment histories."

It's important to remember that your TRW may contain information that you might not see as "credit" information. For instance, it may include records of how promptly you pay your bills. "Students often don't understand what it means to be in a contract," explains Buskirk. "For example, let's say a student has a dispute with her roommates over a long-distance telephone bill. Nobody pays while the argument rages. The problem is that someone is responsible for payment of that bill. If that bill is turned over to a collection agency, it's likely to become part of her credit history." A bill that isn't paid—for whatever reason—is, in effect, a violation of a contract. And credit-card issuers don't want to trust someone who would violate a contract. So this type of short-term dispute could have a long-term effect on your credit history.

Adverse credit information stays on your record for seven years. Sounds awful doesn't it? But it's easy to avoid. Pay your bills on time and don't bounce any checks. Then you won't have to worry about TRW.

O Debt, Where Is Thy Sting?

Let's say you've turned in your application and been approved. The first thing you get is a card . . . and a credit-card agreement. When you're looking over your credit-card agreement, pay close attention to the rate of interest charged for outstanding balances. For most cards this rate is 19.8%—that's 1.65% per month! This can add up to a lot of money. But you don't have to pay this money. If you pay off your balance each month, your credit card is really "plastic money": all the card does is delay your payment a little. But, if you pay off the balance over time, you'll be using the "credit" feature of the card— a loan, which must be paid back with interest.

Let's say that after getting your new credit card, you go out and celebrate. The celebration consists of tapping out your $500 credit line by purchasing a CD player and 20 disks. Using 1.65% per month on the outstanding balance, it will take you 35 months to pay this bill with minimum payments of $20 per month. The total cost will be $706. A finance charge of $206, or over 40% of the original price, over three years! Instant gratification? Yes. Enduring ramifications? Most certainly.

And remember, credit is a privilege and not a right. The issuer may cancel the card at any time. When can a card be canceled? If you fail to meet minimum payments, you can expect your card to be canceled. If you exceed your credit limit, the ax of cancelation may fall. If you're a first-time user of the card and you exceed your limit, you will most likely be canceled. If you have a habit of staying within your credit limit, and you exceed the limit, the issuer may let it pass.

A final word about your fiscal responsibility to yourself regarding your credit card. Bankruptcy attorneys around the country report that credit cards are the major culprits in about 3 to 5% of the cases they see. However, credit cards are almost always part of a credit hole that most folks claiming bankruptcy protection dig for themselves. "For young people a major cause of bankruptcy is an expensive car," says Sam Brugger, of Merriam & Mauch's New Legal Clinic, in Madison, Wisconsin. "However, both young and old fall prey to credit cards. Abuse of credit cards is the serious problem for most people."

Plastic Madness!

When you receive your credit card, it will come with a credit-card agreement and a brochure explaining the features and services

---

HERE'S YOUR CREDIT CARD, WHAT'S YOUR HURRY?

Why do financial institutions fall all over themselves trying to sign students as credit-card holders? Because it's good business.

"Students are better credit risks than the population at large," explains Citibank's Ahearn. "Approximately 4 to 5% of loans to credit cardholders go bad. Yet students have a lower default percentage and they are considered good business."

Since 1983, Citibank has enrolled more than 1.5 million students as credit-card customers. In the early 'eighties, students told Citibank that they needed credit cards to help build a positive credit history. Students also needed a credit limit that would cover the cost of items such as books or airline tickets. So Citibank obliged.

"In most cases this is a student's first credit card," reports Ahearn. "The number of transactions is normally low, and we find that our new cardholders are building experience with the card."

"And these students aren't shy," he continues. "They remind us that when they graduate and enter the work force, they will need car loans, a mortgage for their homes, and investment advice." Giving these customers credit cards while they are students often helps cement a long-term relationship.

offered with your card. The agreement will also explain the finance charges for account balances.

Now that you're the proud holder of a credit card, you ought to know what more it does than just allow you to charge purchases. Depending on the features and services offered with your card, you may be able to:

1. Guarantee accommodations at hotels and motels.
2. Add flight insurance to each airline ticket you purchase.
3. Avoid paying additional insurance when you rent a car.
4. Receive extended warranties on items purchased with the card.

Credit cards can offer a multitude of features. Take a few minutes to review the features that are unique to your card.

Credit-card issuers also offer premium cards, nicknamed, Gold, Platinum, etc. These cards usually carry higher annual fees— in some cases as high as $150. Premium cards are designed primarily for the business traveler. Lost-luggage insurance, medical services in foreign countries, and use of executive travel agencies or services are just some of these features offered to a business traveler. She may need the vast array of features offered through a premium card. You don't.

You are now ready to "master the possibilities." Before you do, perhaps you ought to . . .

Master the Responsibilities

Whether your credit limit is high or low, you must exercise care not to exceed this limit. If you find that you need a bigger credit limit, just ask. After you've used your card for a few months, many issuers will accommodate you. You may also find that credit issuers will automatically raise the limit on your card over time, provided you have developed a good history.

It is also a good idea to save your credit-card receipts until you receive your bill. Then check the receipts against the charges on your bill. Comparing your receipts with the itemized list on your bill will help you discover any erroneous charges.

One other responsibility is reporting your card lost or stolen as soon as you realize this has happened. In your agreement you'll find a toll-free number to call in the event of just such an emergency. You're responsible for the first $50 charged with your card before it is reported lost or stolen. Quick action can save you that $50.

Don't lend the card to anyone. That's like handing someone a blank check. Also, watch the carbons. Some credit-card receipts still have carbon paper between the transaction slips. One slip goes to the bank, the other to the merchant, and the last is your record. Enterprising thieves have gone through the garbage at retailers and restaurants, grabbed the carbons, and—using your number—they have a mail-order feeding frenzy. Most merchants will ask if you want the carbons. Say yes, and destroy them later.

Finally, try to avoid using your credit card to charge purchases over the phone. Yes, Virginia, you can play Santa Claus by ordering over the phone with your credit card. But if someone else has that number, it's open season on your card.

Credit-Card Protection

The nightmare begins when you lose your wallet or purse. Gone are your keys, important telephone number, driver's license, money, all your bank cards and credit cards. Hassle enough. But it's not as bad as it could be. Under the 1969 Truth in Lending Act, you are only liable for the first $50 charged to your credit card prior to notifying the issuer of your loss. And if you discover the loss quickly, you might be able to call the issuer fast enough to prevent losing that $50.

The trick is, you have to know who to call. A simple solution is to make a photocopy of your credit cards. Then write down the toll-free numbers you're supposed to call when notifying the issuer of a loss. If you have only two or three cards, this is a very simple procedure.

Or you can use one of the credit-card protection companies. You would expect Bob May, President of Credit Card Sentinel, to insist that you need credit-card protection. After all, that's what his company does. "We register all of your credit cards," explains May. "If you lose your cards, or they are stolen, you then make one toll-free call—to us. We know how to notify the issuers. It's fast and it's accurate"

This service costs $5. The price of a decent hamburger. Other companies offer the same service, and fees can run anywhere from $5 to $15 a year. May reports that on average most of his customers register about seven cards with Credit Card Sentinel, which protects bank cards as well. But if you have just a few cards, you can perform this service for yourself . . . and have a hamburger, too.

How Much Is Too Much?

How many credit cards should you have? There are advantages and disadvantages to having too few or too many. Having more cards increases your total line of credit. Also, some stores don't accept certain major credit cards. For example, if you only have an American Express card and the merchant you're dealing with does not honor that card, you may have to forgo a purchase. However, there is a disadvantage to having a large number of cards. More cards increase your ability to get into debt. And, if the cards are lost or stolen, it'll be tougher to contain the possible financial damage.

FUSS BUDGET

▼ ▼ ▼

*Kimberly was a member in good standing of the "Shop 'Til You Drop"
brigade. After six months of living in her own apartment, she was
broke. She had a kicky new wardrobe, a state-of-the-art food proces-
sor, and a miniature color TV—but her checking account balance
was down to $4.25 and she'd reached the limits on all her credit
cards. When the rent came due, Kimberly had no money to pay it.*

*Not knowing what else to do, Kimberly phoned her parents to
ask for help. And help came . . . in the form of good advice. She'd
have to pay off her credit cards and give up her apartment.*

*So Kimberly headed home. As she loaded the back seat of her
car with clothes, and the trunk with new gadgets and appliances,
she wondered where all her money had gone. After all, she'd
bought everything on sale!*

Budgeting is the first step to becoming self-sufficient. Setting up and maintaining a realistic budget—one that matches what you spend with what you have available to spend—is a valuable skill. A good budget is really just a means to an end—a plan to help you get what you really need and want, not to prevent you from enjoying life. Developed, written, and then adhered to, a budget can help you achieve your financial goals—and keep you from missing the mark on other goals.

Keep in mind that budgeting is subject to personal style and choice. It's a way for you to set your priorities. You may be more than content eating peanut butter and jelly sandwiches day-in and day-out while your profligate roommate can't survive without surf and turf once a week. Or you may find life without the latest CDs unbearable, while others insist that fashion or travel is a must. The point is, it doesn't matter what your priorities are; what matters is how to make them possible...without sacrificing too much of anything. Skillful budgeting helps you choose the particular luxuries your crave while maintaining the necessities.

Everybody has to budget. Donald Trump somehow has to make it on only $450,000 a month. Even corporations have to budget. One top executive we know chooses to fly commercial rather than using her company's private jet. The cost of the private jet for a Los Angeles-to-New York is $15,349. The price of a round-trip, first-class ticket on a major airline is between $1,000 and $1,850.

So, how do you draw up a budget, determine what is and isn't within your means, estimate how much to set aside for emergencies, and learn how to stretch the dollar to get more "bang for the buck"?

Building Blocks

From the early days of radio to the hottest new sit-com, budgets and the failure to stick to them have been the staple for comedy writers. But all kidding aside, devising and sticking to a good budget will prevent your own finances from becoming grist for future sit-coms.

To prepare a simple budget, you need to identify all sources of income and all anticipated expenses. So grab some paper and a pencil. Make sure the pencil has an eraser; any good budget will allow for adjustments.

Here are the three steps to budgeting.

Step One: Income

How you're going to spend, or allocate, your money depends on how much you have. That should be easy enough. Start by identifying all your sources of income: allowance from home; grants; student loans; gifts from grandparents, friends, or relatives; interest on checking or savings accounts; money earned at work; and so forth. Then list each source, one by one.

Take Jane, for example. Jane's parents have agreed to give her $500 each semester. She's found a part-time word-processing job that will clear $135 a week. She also has a savings account of $3,000, which gives her a quarterly interest payment of $45. Now Jane can build an income statement, being careful to itemize what money she'll receive and when she'll receive it. Here's what the first three months might look like:

September	
Parent's gift	$500
Savings interest	45
Job salary	540
Total	$1,085

October	
Job salary	$540

November	
Job salary	$540
First three months' income	$2,165

Jane now has a good idea how much money she'll have—and when it'll be available—for the first three months of the school year.

Now consider Dick. Dick works part-time for a food-catering service. He makes $6 an hour, and he usually works 15 hours a week. After taxes, he makes about $75 each week. Dick's grandmother gives him $100 each month for school. Dick has also saved $2,400 from summer jobs, which he plans to use during the school year. Here's what his three-month income statement might look like:

September	
Job salary	$300
Grandmother's gift	$100
Monthly depletion of savings	$240
Total	$640

October/November

NOTE: Dick's income for October and November will the same, $640 each month $1,280

First three months' income $1,920

Step Two: Outgo

Now do some more brainstorming. Take a few minutes to identify all the things you might spend money on, and write each one down. Most people don't really understand the costs of living on their own until they've moved out of their parents' house. Common expenses include:

Rent	Telephone
Food	Electric/Gas
Tuition	Cable TV

Water
Books
Clothing allowance
Shoes
Entertainment
Gifts
Car payment
Parking
Car maintenance and
  repairs
Gasoline and oil for car
Auto insurance
Laundry

Medical/dental
  expense
Haircuts
Transportation (bus, subway,
  train, etc.)
Newspaper
Typing fees
Fraternity/sorority dues
Magazine subscriptions
Traveling home
Computer costs
"Pin money/mad money/
  walking-around money"

You won't necessarily encounter, or deal with, all these expenses. You may need to add an expense that you haven't found on this list. The important thing is to try to identify *all* of your expenses . . . it's easy to overlook the "incidentals."

Continuing with our examples, let's get back to Jane and Dick. Assume that Jane is living off-campus in an apartment. Her share of the rent is $175. Utilities, which include gas and electric, telephone, cable TV, and possibly water, run about $110 a month, of which Jane pays half. She owns her car outright and has estimated that gas, oil, insurance, and maintenance run about $100 a month. She figures that her food bill will be $100 each month. Laundry is relatively inexpensive—Jane uses the machines in the laundry room of her apartment complex—and along with some drycleaning, the monthly is $25. She gets the local newspaper, $8 a month. Haircuts are $12. The on-campus parking sets her back $60 for the semester. Books for the first semester are $213. Clothes are also a consideration, as well as a considerable expense. Wearing the latest fashions on campus can set a person back more than a few dollars. But Jane's just a modest clothes horse; she's budgeted $100 per month. Now, let's see how she fared:

JANE

Semester expenses

Books..$213

Parking.. 60
                                                        =====

Total.. $273

Monthly expenses:

Rent.. $175

Utilities.. 55

Car.. 100

Food.. 100

Clothes.. 100

Drycleaning.. 25

Newspaper.. 8

Haircut.. 12
                                                        =====

Total monthly expenses.. $575

                                                            X3

Three months' expenses............................... $1,725
                                                        =====

Semester and monthly total........................... $1,998

Dick lives alone in an apartment; the rent is $225. His utilities run $85, including cable TV with a premium station at $35 a month. He walks to school and work. Dick's food bill is $150 a month, and he also spends $30 each month on protein supplements and vitamins. His haircuts cost $6 and he goes to the barber about once a month. Dick drops his entire bag of dirty clothes at the laundry, which charges him $40 each month. His book bill is $275 for the first semester. Dick has subscribed to *Sports Illustrated, Time,* and *TV Guide* for the first semester at a cost of $50. He's hard on shoes, so he plans to buy a new pair of Nike's for $85. Dick doesn't care at all about clothes; he's happy in jeans and tee shirts, but he's budgeted $50 a month. Let's see how Dick fared:

DICK
Semester expenses

Books..$275

Shoes.. 85

Magazines.. 50

Total.. $410

Monthly expenses

Rent.. $225

Utilities.. 85

Food.. 150

Protein/Vitamins.. 30

Clothing allowance... 50

Laundry.. 40

Haircut.. 6

Total monthly expenses... $586

x3

Three month expenses.. $1,758

Semester and monthly total.. $2,168

Budgets are hard to work out in your head. Write everything down. You don't need a 13-column spreadsheet, or Lotus 1-2-3 on your computer to keep an accurate budget and record of expenditures. Work out your own system. Take a spiral notebook. On the left-hand page, log in your income. On the right-hand page, record expenses. Whenever you go to the grocery store, or grab a meal at a restaurant, that goes under "Food." The cable television bill goes under "Utilities." You don't need to be an economist; just be thorough.

Step Three: Making Choices

OK, you've got all this wonderful information. How do you use it?

The first thing you do with it is to compare your outgo with your income. Then you use your comparison to make some choices. Budgets often boil down to trade-offs.

In our first example, Jane has an income of $2,165 and expenses of $1,998 for the first three months of the school year. This gives her a surplus of $167. This money is her "discretionary income"; she can spend it on whatever she pleases.

If Jane decided that she didn't need a car, she would save $100 each month and the $60 per semester parking fee. The trade-off may be the cost of public transportation, usually at a student discount, or biking or walking to and from school. Rather than having $167 in discretionary income, she would have $527. Now she has more choices. She might choose to move into a larger, better apartment. She might update her wardrobe. She might buy a new stereo system. Or she just might want to build up her savings.

One of the benefits of this comparison exercise is that you may discover that some of the "necessities" are not as crucial as you once thought. That's what Dick has realized. His outgo for the first three months exceeds his budgeted income by $248. He has three options: to tap into his savings, to cut expenses, or to get more hours at work. Dick needs his savings, so he takes a close look at his expenses. Not renewing *TV Guide* will save $15. By doing his own laundry at a laundromat, Dick can save $25 each month. He also finds that he really doesn't have the time to watch much TV, so he gives up his cable, saving $35 a month. These choices will save Dick $195. He's still $53 over budget, so he plans to work a few more hours each week.

Use a budget to cover necessities first, luxuries later.

Emergency!

Ideally, you should have sufficient funds set aside in case of an emergency. To plan how much money you need, ask yourself this question: "What's the worst thing that could happen to me?" What if a family member is seriously ill or dies, and you have to travel home? What if you break an ankle playing intramural basketball and can't work for two months? What if you lose your job?

The money that you would need to carry you through these dilemmas is your emergency fund.

Financial planners recommend that you have enough money saved to cover three to six months of expenses. Again, following our examples, Jane would need about $1,725 in her emergency fund, while Dick would need $1,758. This will help them weather a rather severe financial storm.

If you don't have the financial resources to make it through an emergency, you might turn to your parents or relatives for an emergency loan. Some schools will lend students money to pay to get home during a family crisis. You might also use the credit line on your charge card.

Tricks of the Trade

Now that you've got a budget, here are a few tricks of the trade that will help stay within that budget. Remember, the more you save on necessities, the more you'll have for savings and luxury items.

USED BOOKS Some college bookstores, and many bookstores in college areas, offer used textbooks for sale. The savings on used books could be as much as 50%. But watch out! Make certain you buy the correct edition. The 10th edition will do you little good if the rest of the class is reading and studying the 11th.

FURNITURE One of the great adventures of living on your own is furnishing your first apartment. Consider an "eclectic decor," often dubbed "early flea market." Standard college furniture leans toward cable-reel tables and cinder block and board bookshelves. You can paint cinder blocks any color you like, and stain and varnish the boards. Or you can cover your boards in burlap. The point is that you don't need an Ethan Allen bedroom suite or American Drew dining room sets for a successful college career. (Hint: Your relatives are terrific sources of old furniture. Take a tour of family attics and basements before departing for school.)

COUPONS Spend a few minutes with the Sunday newspaper inserts and clip coupons for groceries and sundries. One dollar off a box of detergent is a nice savings. And watch for stores that offer double coupons. In the competitive grocery business, many stores actually refund twice the stated coupon value. Let's say you have a coupon for $1 off three packages of macaroni and cheese. The packages cost 99 cents each, and the store doubles the coupon. Total cost is $2.97; the coupon, doubled, is $2—you pay 97 cents for the three packages! Food, desserts, detergents, soaps, paper products, over-the-counter medicines, household items—there are coupons for all this stuff. Clip 'em and save money. (Coupon warning: Don't buy a product simply because you have a coupon. What good is $5 off on a 50 lb. bag of Kennel Ration if you don't own a dog?)

STUDENT DISCOUNTS Ask merchants if they offer a student discount. Many movie theatres, restaurants, and bookstores offer student discounts. Some cities offer student discounts on public transportation. The savings can be significant, but you won't know unless you ask. And when you ask, be prepared to provide a current student ID card. (Robert Townsend, producer/writer/director of the movie "Hollywood Shuffle," once bought film and equipment at a student discount merely by wearing a UCLA sweatshirt! But you might not be so lucky.)

GENERICS Generic products have pushed some name brands off the shelves by appealing to the cost-conscious. Aspirin, ibuprofen, prescription drugs, blue jeans, knit shirts, and canned vegetables are just a few of the "no-name brand" items available. The difference between a Ralph Lauren knit shirt and a "generic" knit can be $10 or more. That's a lot of money for a little polo player.

TWO-FERS Take advantage of "two-for-the-price-of-one"

offers. You can find these in newspapers and in special coupon books such as *Entertainment* or *Let's Dine Out*. *Entertainment* offers discount books for nearly 100 cities in the U.S. and Canada. Savings are offered for dining out in fine restaurants, noshing at a deli, and even pigging out at fast food joints. Discounts on sporting events, movies, recreational facilities, and hotels are also included. These books can save many times their purchase price.

BARGAINING Don't be afraid to bargain. Some merchants may give a discount for paying in cash rather than using a credit card. Cash is king, and in that gray area between wholesale (what the merchant pays for goods) and retail (what you pay), a lot of savings await the bold souls willing to bargain. Again, you won't know until you ask. (Hint: Gas stations often offer discounts for cash.)

SELLING YOUR OLD STUFF Think of selling your old stuff as financial recycling. Sell your old books, clothes, furniture, and appliances. Sure, you won't get a king's ransom for that cable reel table, but any amount is better than throwing it out. Flea markets, swap meets, garage sales, and even a bit of campus retailing (through advertisements in the school paper or well-placed index cards) can bring in a modest windfall.

CASH Keep only as much cash as you need. Try this little experiment. Take $40 from the cash machine and try to make it last a week. Then take $100 and try to make it last a week. You'll probably finish each week with about the same amount of money in your pockets. Money follows some strange, immutable law. Whatever you have in your wallet seems to escape, no matter how much or how little. By keeping just the necessary cash on hand, you'll control your spending. There's a lesson here. With ready cash, a magazine and an ice cream cone are tempting, and certainly within your means, a mere $4 indulgence! But it's hard to buy when you aren't awash in cash. Try to avoid impulse buying. Why do you think you are flanked by the *National Enquirer, People, Cosmopolitan,* candy bars, batteries, cigarettes, and gum while you're in the check-out line at the grocery store? You really don't need these items for your survival, but they're just so handy.

The Moral to the Story: A Car in Cheryl's Garage

Still not convinced that setting up a budget, sticking to it, and finding ways to save money are worth your time? Well, then, let's take the case of Cheryl. Cheryl used grocery store coupons to reduce her food bill, but her roommate just wasn't convinced that it was saving Cheryl any money. "So I opened a savings account," said Cheryl, "and I saved all the money from the cents-off coupons." Cheryl says she didn't turn into some raving coupon-clipping lunatic with a pair of scissors in each hand. She merely used coupons for items she normally purchased. In two and half years she saved enough to buy . . . a car!

Look for ways to make and save money—spending it is always very easy.

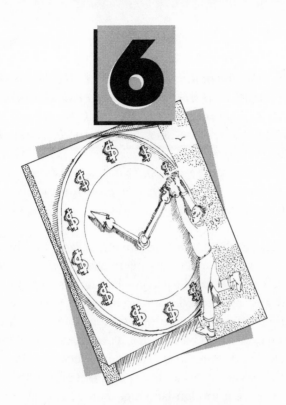

TIME IS MONEY

▼ ▼ ▼

*Jeff was baffled by the poor grades he received during his first
semester in college. He had always been a good student in high
school. "I don't understand it," he moaned. "I spend four hours in
the library almost every day, and I don't feel like I get anything
accomplished."*

*The mystery wasn't solved until his sister, who was one year
behind him in school, started classes at the same university. She
observed Jeff's evening sojourns into the halls of learning and
reported the results. "Jeff would get to the library and spend 15
minutes arranging his books, sharpening his pencils, and laying
out his 13 colored highlighting pens. Then he'd go to the bathroom.
When he got back, he'd read four pages of* The Great Gatsby. *Then
he'd get a Coke. On the way back to his table, he'd meet a friend*

and talk for half an hour. Then he'd go to the bathroom again. When he got back, he'd sit down and do a calculus problem, and then immediately get up to search the stacks for a book he needed for his sociology term paper. Then he'd get another Coke. Then he'd hit the bathroom again . . . ."

Four hours in the library isn't always four hours of work. Jeff crammed 12 minutes of studying into those four hours. And he got 12 minutes' worth of results.

As a college student, you'll be leaving behind a fairly structured world. So far, your life has been controlled by others. Your parents have dictated rules for you—laid down curfews, and both encouraged and monitored your homework. Your teachers have set the rules at school—establishing standards and requirements in your coursework. And chances are, your high school curriculum was fairly standard. Sure, you had some electives, but your core courses were carved in stone: four years of English, three years of math, two years of a foreign language, three years of science, and all the stuff you need to get into college.

Now you're on your own. You call the shots and make all the decisions. You're juggling 18 semester hours, a job, perhaps a sport, and an active social life. And your workload is mind-boggling! Two 20-page term papers, a massive laboratory project, and 300 pages of Thomas Wolfe to read by Friday! There just don't seem to be enough hours in a day. Suddenly, time is precious.

While the value of time can be measured in many ways, one of the most common is to remember the truism: "Time is money." As you enter various professions, you'll begin to see a quantitative relationship between time and money. Successful corporate attorneys charge $200+ an hour for their counsel. Advertising executives bill clients monthly using a log to detail their creative efforts. Doctors charge $75 for an office visit. Dental technicians can make $40+ an hour cleaning teeth. Young accountants must prove that they have spent 40 billable hours per week on client matters. Sales representatives who earn $100,000 a year estimate that they earn $50 an hour. A masseuse charges $45 for an hour-long massage.

And a minimum wage laborer earns just under $5 an hour. Yes, time is money.

For many students, college is the first time they wrestle with time-management problems. What are the usual ways students procrastinate? What are colleges and universities doing to help students take control of their time? How do you create and what is the value of a time log? Finally, how do goals play a big part in time-management strategy?

What, Me Worry?

According to campus-based time management experts, it's not the marginal student who usually has problems with time management. On the contrary, it's often those who are motivated and have high self-expectations who have the most difficulty. At Florida State University in Tallahasee, Delcine Townes, MSW and specialist in student counseling, sees many high school honor role students walk through her door. "These kids earned 4.0's in high school," she says, "but the competition wasn't that stiff and they knew how to get by. Now they've completed their first semester and their grade point average ranges between 1.9 and 2.6. Quite frankly, they're in shock!"

Townes points out that problems generally pop up in three areas: old high school study skills no longer work, workloads are heavier than expected, and students have trouble balancing their social life with academic demands.

The techniques students use for success in high school don't always lead to success in college. Many high school students, for example, find it fairly easy to cram for a test in one night. But one-night cram sessions can't guarantee good results in most college courses.

In addition, students often underestimate their workloads. Nancy Nyhan, Assistant Director of the Undergraduate Resource Center at Boston University, also teaches a workshop on time management. She says that students often:

1. Think they can do more in a given time frame than they actually can.
2. Think that the work will be easier than it actually is.
3. Overcommit themselves to projects and activities.
4. Fail to set aside sufficient time to complete papers and prepare for examinations.

Finally, there's all that glorious freedom, which can be a problem. "In college, although they take their work seriously," Townes says, "the kids want to socialize and build new friendships. They have to realize that now, with the workload they have, they just can't do it all."

Students find this balancing act overwhelming, and they start to procrastinate. Here's her favorite sampling of common collegiate procrastinations:

"I think I'll go to the party first, I'll be more in the mood to study later."

"I studied hard for the last test and I did poorly, so what's the use? I know I won't do well this time."

"I know that I could have done well...if I'd only invested the time."

"I don't think I'm smart enough. It's just too difficult. Boy, I must have fooled everybody in high school!"

"I'm going to wait until I get inspired. I work a lot faster that way."

Most of these excuses are just misunderstandings—misunderstandings of the difference between *wasting* time and *managing* it.

The Numbers Never Lie

How do you move from wasting time to managing time? The first step in gaining control over your time is to look at how you're spending it right now.

Bill Hermann, who has taught time management as part of the Dale Carnegie Sales Course, recommends the use of a time log.

▼ *So what's a time log?*
It's a record of your day's activities broken down into short intervals, like 15 minutes.

▼ *Doesn't keeping a time log add to your workload?*
It doesn't take much time to keep the time log . . . maybe five minutes a day when it's all said and done.

▼ *How do you make a time log?*
Making a time log is very simple. Take a sheet of paper and write down times in 15-minute intervals; that is, keep track of your waking hours: 6:00 AM, 6:15 AM, 6:30 AM...11:30 PM. You get the idea. Write these times in columns on your piece of paper, leaving enough room to jot down a word or two next to each time slot.

Each 15 minutes, write down what it is you're doing: "reading the paper," "shower," "breakfast," "Geology class," "BS-ing with Ralph," "Calculus homework," and so on.

▼ *What do you have when you're done keeping this time log?*
A great sense of just how much time you've been wasting.

"Students should keep a time log for two weeks," recommends Hermann. "The first few days they'll lie to themselves."

When Jeff kept his time log, he doubted its value. He really buckled down those first few days, and every time slot demonstrated to him that he was productive. By the third day, Jeff's old habits began to intrude, less work was accomplished, and his sense of frustration returned.

"It's human nature," says Hermann. "Students won't face up to the fact that they're wasting a lot of time on unproductive activities. But, after a few days, honesty makes it debut and that's when the time log really becomes valuable."

After keeping a time log for two weeks, you can review the results. Hermann suggests that you also have someone skilled in time management review the time log and offer advice. The results will be telling; if presented honestly, they could be critical in helping you gain control of your time.

Here's what Jeff found out about his use of time after keeping his log for two weeks. His morning ritual of eating breakfast, reading the newspaper, and watching a morning news program devoured about two hours each day. He used the time between classes to shoot the breeze with his friends, effectively losing another two hours. Intramural sports filled the time between 3:00 and 5:00, but Jeff was always ready to shoot some baskets with other gym rats until dinner time. His four hours in the library "studying" were wasted. This great myth was debunked when he discovered that he spent over an hour hanging out at the Coke machine, 20 minutes arranging his books, and another hour socializing.

Jeff learned a lot the first time he kept a time log, and he cleaned up his act. But after a few months, he fell back into his old ways. Use the time log like a "pop quiz" for your own time management. You need to spring these time logs on yourself at least a couple of times a year to help keep any backsliding in check.

Setting Goals

Goal-setting is a critical step in time management. Champions in sports set goals. The glamour of winning a gold medal in the Olympics overshadows the hard work it took to win it. The marathon runner puts in hard, punishing workouts on the track running sprints. It makes him a better runner. With the gold medal as a dream, it's easier to stay, literally, on "track." Winners in school also set goals. The valedictorian often pushes herself to study that chapter one last time before the test. With the prospect of being accepted by the best schools in the country, it's easier to burn the midnight oil.

Hyrum Smith, President of The Franklin International Institute, Inc., has taught the principles of time management to corporate executives and students. "For goals to work," Smith says, "they must be *specific, measurable,* and *fixed in time.* 'I want to lose weight' is not a goal. 'I want to lose 5 pounds' is not a goal. 'I want to lose 5 pounds by February 1, 199X' is a goal." It's specific . . . 5 pounds. It's measurable . . . on a scale. And it's fixed in time . . . by February 1, 199X.

Once the goals are set, a daily task list must be created. These tasks should be directed toward achieving your goals. Here's an example. Say you want to be an excellent student. How can you achieve that as a goal? Excellence is measured by your grade point average. So, a long-range goal might be to get an "A" in your European History class. Intermediate goals may involve completing a 50-page term paper, performing well on announced quizzes and tests, and completing the text. Daily tasks are then planned: go to the library to check source material on the Battle of Waterloo for your term paper; read pages 345 through 390 and prepare for quiz; and review notes from last week's classes.

So, by diligently completing the daily tasks, you accomplish the intermediate goals, which helps you achieve the long-range goal. Huh? In other words, if you do all your reading and class preparation on schedule, you'll get better grades on quizzes and tests. If you spend time at the library with the material on the Battle of Waterloo when you said you would, you're more likely to have a well-researched term paper. Higher grades on the quizzes, tests, and term paper will help you get the "A."

But you must plan for this success. "I recommend that you take 15 to 20 minutes each day for planning," says Smith. "It is critical that you do this planning alone and in a quiet place with no distractions."

Beware...You may create conflicting goals. In your enthusiasm to commit goals to paper and begin achieving them, you can often lose sight of the fact that you may be biting off more than you can chew. As Boston University's Nyhan points out, "Students overcommit themselves. It just may not be possible to take a full courseload, work a part-time job, and be on the tennis team. You may actually do these three demanding undertakings, but you won't do them well."

Scoring Goals

Here are some other tips from the mavens of time management, techniques that will help you in taking control.

CHUNKING Chunking—breaking a large task down into smaller "chunks"—works on any large project. Take the awesome and reduce it to the do-able. Suppose you're out on an 8-mile run. You can "fool" yourself by breaking the run down into more manageable chunks. Run to a point 2 miles from the start; then, knowing you've completed a quarter of your run, you "decide" whether or not to press on. At the half-way point, you've done another chunk; now you know that it's psychologically (and in reality) all downhill. Soon enough, with every landmark you pass farther down the road, you chew up the 8 miles. This concept can be used with any large project, like reading *War and Peace* (1433 pages in paperback), writing a 25-page term paper, painting a house, writing a book, or making your first million.

BRAINSTORMING You "brainstorm" by tossing out all the ideas you can about a project or task, paying little regard to sequence or logic. For example, you've been told that you will be given an exam in your European History class two weeks from today. How do you prepare for the exam? You just write down everything you can think of that will help you. Your list may include such items as "review class notes," "re-read Chapters 1 through 7," "discuss the War of the Roses with study group," and "outline succession to the British throne." Then you schedule these tasks over the next two weeks, thus making your exam preparation logical—and taking control.

LASER THINKING A laser is a highly concentrated beam of light which can actually cut steel. Laser thinking, then, is focusing your efforts and energy on the task at hand. Here's how Jeff, our wayward library visitor, would use laser thinking. He could read the assigned pages of *Gatsby* and get them done. Then he could turn to calculus next and hammer out the problems. Finally, he could check the stacks for the sociology books he needs for his term paper. By getting "a job" done, you can then move ahead to accomplish the others.

THE STUDY HAT In my college days I wore a study hat. It was a beat-up brown fedora, very dramatic and totally out of fashion. But when I put it on, it was a sign to my roommates that I was getting down to business. I also respected the power of the hat. When I studied, I wore it; when I was finished, off it came. Many time-management gurus recommend using something crazy like a study hat when you are focusing on getting things done.

Variations of the study hat may be a special chair, a certain pen, or some other magical talisman that you use only when you study.

MO' BETTER TIPS

1. Find out if you're a morning person or a night person. Then concentrate your studying during your times of peak efficiency.
2. Alternate the subject matter of your class schedule. Statistics followed by differential equations can be exhausting. Try to mix a literature class between those mathematics courses and give the other side of your brain a rest.
3. Make sure that you schedule breaks. If you overload and burn out, you'll lose valuable time.

And Now for Something Completely Different

Reward yourself. Giving yourself a "prize" for a job well done is important. The rewards can be simple: a piece of cheesecake, a can of Diet Coke, watching Sportscenter on ESPN for a half an hour, or just being lazy. Rewards for significant achievements should be more dramatic. Throw a party, plan a special night, buy a new outfit. Celebrate. These celebrations reinforce the good time-management habits and the successes they engender. Besides, they're fun.

"By completing the daily tasks, students become empowered," says Hyrum Smith. "They experience success with control.

Daily successes help build self-esteem and lead to bigger victories. We call it the 'lantern' theory. A lantern throws off a pool of light, and by raising the lantern you can explore to the edges of the pool. But each advance then allows you to continue advancing right to the edge of the forest by just lifting that lantern again and again."

By following these suggestions you become *proactive* rather than *reactive*. Proactive students are the ones who have read and reviewed the material for a test, studied it over a period of time. Reactive students swallow handfuls of No-Doz and pull all-nighters.

You can't control everything in your life. Time management is about getting control over the things you can.

THE LOAN
ARRANGER

▼ ▼ ▼

In my sophomore year in high school, a quartet of seniors made
the rounds just before Easter recess, asking for our spare change.
Using a variation of "Brother, can you spare a dime?" they man-
aged to collect over $125. At the end of the school day, the soon-to-
graduate panhandlers hopped into a late '60s Rambler and spent
their spring break in Fort Lauderdale.

Needless to say, they never paid a penny of the money back.

The next year I found myself as the school's Commissioner of
Finance, which meant that I was saddled with something called
the Student Loan Program. This was a very simple, yet high-mind-
ed idea. Funded by $300 in sock-hop profits, the Student Loan Pro-

gram lent money to students who had a need. The normal loan was $5 to $25 and could be used to buy books, school supplies, or even to help pay tuition. These loans were supposed to be paid back, of course, along with a modest interest charge. Theoretically, the interest would keep the program's coffers full, while teaching the students fiscal responsibility.

We didn't have any trouble making loans. We just doled out the money on a first-come, first-served basis. Most of the loans were made, in fact, to the "greaser" element of the student body and the proceeds used to buy cigarettes and carburetors . . . probably for late '60s Ramblers.

I learned a big lesson later that year as I lost the election for Student Council Vice President. Never lend money to anyone who's a lousy credit risk.

At some point one of your friends, classmates, or even a casual college acquaintance will hit you up for a loan. Perhaps on another occasion it may be you searching an empty wallet or purse.

Are there different kinds of loans? Should I feel obligated to lend someone money? What do I do if they don't pay me back? How do I know when and when not to lend money? What do I do if I have to borrow?

Informal borrowing—between friends and acquaintances—is part of life. People will ask you for money. How you handle their request will determine whether you're a soft touch, a shrewd businessperson, or a friend in deed.

The Three Types of Loans

"Neither a borrower nor a lender be;
For loan oft loses both itself and friend . . ."
SHAKESPEARE: *Hamlet*, I, iii, 75

Good advice. A little impractical maybe, and against your kindhearted and generous nature, but sound advice. Your dad might have told you never to lend money to friends or relatives. (Your dad always seems to have a plethora of advice he's willing to heap on you.) In this case the old man is right. Why? The fact is, you can never guarantee that a loan will be repaid.

How a loan is repaid, or *not* repaid, determines what kind of loan it is. For example, your buddy Pete makes a request for a loan. "Hey, Paul," he says, "I'm really in a bind. I don't get paid until Friday and I need $20 to hold me over." You've got the $20, and, well, Pete's been an OK guy and you think he'll probably pay the money back. So you hand him the $20.

So, you've just given Pete a loan. Now, depending on what happens next, you may find out what kind of loan you made. There are three types.

"LOAN AS A LOAN"   In this case, Paul pays you back that weekend, early in the next week, or the first time you see him after his Friday payday. In other words, it's paid back on time and in full. Painless! And, you were able to help a buddy out.

"LOAN AS A GIFT"   Pete sees you catching rays on Saturday morning and comes up to you and says "Paul, I've got that $20 for you." If you tell Pete to forget it or to hold on to it until you might need a little help, you've effectively converted it into a gift. Any time you consciously forgive a debt, of your own volition, it should be considered a gift.

"LOAN AS A LOSS"   If Pete suddenly begins to duck you, forget your name, continually use the excuse that he's forgotten his wallet, then your loan is beginning to look like a big mistake. You suddenly hear that Pete has hit on two-thirds of your classmates for loans and owes thousands. This is a "loan as a loss"—whenever the other person decides that he's not going to pay you back." Got it? If *you* decide, it's a gift. If *he* decides, it's a loss.

Assessing the Credit Risk

Who exactly do you lend money to and how can you be reasonably sure of getting it back? Imagine this. You walk into five banks, ask who the loan officers are, and ask them if they'll lend you twenty bucks. Chances are you'll be escorted out of each bank by a dour bank guard. Before a banker will lend you money, he has to be reasonably certain that you will pay it back; in other words, that you are a good credit risk. The banker will require that you fill out forms detailing your financial history. He will ask for credit references, and he will be interested specifically in loans that you have received and then paid back. He will check those references. Generally, he will ask for collateral—something of value you give in exchange for the loan. Granted, all this would be a bit much for a measly twenty bucks, but you get the message. You have to use the same discipline when you are asked for a loan by a friend or family member.

Is he creditworthy? Let's resurrect Pete. If you know that Pete is fairly reliable, has a job, and has paid back other people he's borrowed money from, then he makes a good credit risk. On the other hand, if the word is out that Pete welshes on bets, owes money up and down the campus, has 36 parking tickets, and generally does wind sprints whenever he sees the campus police, he's not a good credit risk.

Perhaps Pete is new to your circle of friends or merely an acquaintance and he hasn't yet developed a reputation for reliability. Researching a history file with references is both awkward and impractical. Instead, rely more on intuition in situations that are difficult to read.

What's the reason for the loan? The reason Pete is borrowing the money may be critical in your decision whether to lend him the money. Try to find out what the money will be used for. If the money is going to be used for something important, you're more likely to make the loan. Books, food, repairs for the car, rent, and other necessities are legitimate needs of all students that at some time become extraordinary expenses impossible to budget.

It's not always possible to ascertain the reason for a loan. It might just be too personal for the person to divulge. He might also be lying to you, claiming that the money is needed for rent and then returning with two tickets to the Van Halen concert. Common

"I'VE GOT A BAD FEELING ABOUT THIS . . ."

If you feel that you are being cornered by a loan request, that you would rather not part with the gelt, but don't have a reason handy to deny the loan, then stop right there! You've picked up signals from your wannabe borrower regarding his creditworthiness, but your mind hasn't processed them logically yet. You sense that this is going to be a bad loan. So, have some responses at the ready:

"I wish I could help you out but I'm scraping by as it is..."

Or...

"I know I look rich with this wad in my hand, but it's already spoken for . . ."

Or...

"Tell you what, let me make a list of my bills coming up and I'll see if I have money to spare..."

In all three instances you've been gracious but you've sent a clear message: Find another target.

sense applies. Use what evidence is available.

When will the loan be paid back? Another good policy is to set a payback period for the loan. For small loans, a fairly short time frame is best. "Next week...next Friday...the 15th..." etc. For larger loans, you may actually want to set up a payback period. I once sold a very used Fiat convertible to a friend who was a bit pressed for cash. I asked that he pay me $100 a month for five months on the first day of each month until the car was paid for...the sale price was $500. The risk was that this very used Fiat would explode on the road and my friend would refuse to pay. Neither happened.

In summary, then, try to apply some of the discipline a banker would use in making a loan: the reputation ("creditworthiness") of the borrower, the reason for the loan, and when it will paid back. A final word to the wise: If the loan becomes a loss, a write-off (or "write-down" in bank parlance), you'll also lose a friend. That's the only guarantee in the lending business.

Bad Judgment

Not every loan you make will work out as planned. Some loans that you make will not be paid back, or not paid back in full. In certain situations, you may have legal recourse. Personal loans, both written and oral, are legal, binding contracts. The failure to repay a loan is considered a breach of contract. But since personal loans are more than likely for a nominal amount, any legal action would probably be restricted to Small Claims Court. And oral contracts are hard to prove; it's obviously easier to prove that a contract exists if you produce a written agreement.

But let's be realistic. You probably won't ask a friend to write out an IOU for $25. You probably won't drag a friend into Small Claims Court to recover $25. It's a hassle. Most likely, what will happen is that you'll lose the friend. If every conversation you two have begins with your question "Hey, where's the $25 you owe me?" she ends up avoiding you and you end up distrusting her. Hardly the basis for a good friendship.

How to Ask for a Loan

What if it's you who needs a loan? Then just apply the same principles. In reverse. By paying back small loans promptly, you will establish a reputation as a good credit risk. Always pay the loan back *before* your friend asks for her money. If you run into a problem, let her know as soon as possible. Establish a strong need for the money and also set a definite time for repayment. It goes a little like this.

"Kathy, I need a big favor. My car's in the shop and it needs a new battery. I'm a little short of cash right now and I'd like to know if you could lend me $35. I'll pay you back next Friday when my check from home comes."

Admit it, isn't it a lot better than "Yo, Kathy! You got $35 I can have?"

WORKIN'

▼ ▼ ▼

Brad was determined to get a college education, but didn't know how he was going to pay for it. He wanted to earn enough money working during the summer to carry him through the upcoming academic year. "I don't care what kind of job it is," he mused, "just as long as it's legal and it pays a lot." A friend told him about a job in Alaska. The work would be repetitious, but the pay was great. Actually, the more Brad heard about the job, the better it sounded. He would be working with people his own age. They'd all live together in a bunkroom. Share meals. Sort of like summer camp!

Brad wound up working at a salmon cannery in Alaska—on the "slime line." The slime line was definitely an "entry-level position." Brad worked twelve-hour days for eight

*weeks. It was mind-numbing, back-breaking, filthy work sepa-
rating the edible from the inedible on thousands of salmon.
"Repetitious" was the least of Brad's concerns. But at summer's
end he had made $10,000.*

Many of you will choose to work while you're in college,
maybe part-time during the school year, or full-time while
attending night classes or just during summer vacation. Some of
you will work to supplement your income, others for experience,
or possibly a little bit of both.

How do you identify your reasons for working and how do
you set the priorities? Are you working for maximum income or just
for the experience? What do employers look for in a resume and an
application? How can you make your resume more convincing?
How can you find out what jobs are available? How do you negotiate for a better salary and other benefits?

A lot of factors go into finding the right job. Once you begin
the job hunt, don't have any illusions. The novelty of meeting all of
those "nice people" and learning about those "interesting companies" wears off quickly. Frankly, it's a tedious, frustrating, and often
humbling experience. But, like everything else worthwhile in life,
hard work can reward you big time!

Getting Your Priorities Straight

The first question you should ask yourself is "Why am I working?"
The knee-jerk answer will most likely be "Money!" Then you have
to ask "What kind of job am I looking for?" You blurt out with impa-
tience, "Any job!"

In fact, the answers to these questions are not as obvious as
you might think. As you begin your job search, you'll find that seriously considering these questions may help you focus on the right
job. The answers you come up with now may save you time as
well as the frustration of pursuing leads that just don't make sense
for you.

Let's look at some factors you should consider before searching for a job:

MONEY If your reason for working is to finance your college education, then top dollar is the ultimate priority. Like Brad's job on the slime line, the least "appetizing" jobs often pay the most. You might think about a job in construction, or waiting tables, detailing cars, and for the exceptional salesperson, selling encyclopedias door-to-door.

CONVENIENCE If you're in search of the generic, yellow-label JOB, then convenience may be the critical element. For example, maybe it's just more convenient to work at the video rental store two blocks from your dorm. Working close to where you live has other advantages. If it takes you 40 minutes to commute one-way to your job, you're adding almost an hour and a half to your workday—without compensation.

FIELD OF INTEREST Your main priority may be to garner valuable experience that will apply to your career. If you're considering a career in advertising, for example, you might take a non-paying position as a "go-fer" in an ad agency. You're sacrificing current earnings for experience, but this may pay off handsomely when it comes time to apply for the real job. If you rely on your earnings for living expense, this is not the option for you.

FLEXIBLE HOURS Flexible hours could determine your choice of a job. Two jobs may offer similar pay and benefits, and require comparable skills. The one that fits your schedule best may get the nod.

SKILL DEVELOPMENT Besides a check, what do you want to get out of a job? Perhaps you want to learn what it's like to manage, or work in a team environment, or work independently. Maybe you'd like to develop strong communications skills, or build some customer relations experience. Even when a job is not directly related to your field of interest, you'll find that many skills are transferable and "work" for you as you advance in your career.

Okay. Now that you've determined why you're working, we come to the next critical step: how to get a job. And that means marketing—marketing *you*.

The New and Improved Me!

"I tell students to think of their resumes as TV commercials," says Pam Gardner, Associate Director of the Center for Career Development at the University of Vermont. "Know your product inside and out, highlight all its benefits, target your audience, then market it like mad!"

A resume is the *"Reader's Digest"* version of your life. A resume describes who you are, what you've done, and where you've been educated. In addition to the job application, it is your introduction to the employer.

Gardner reports that according to a number of studies conducted by universities, a prospective employer spends just 20-30 seconds reviewing a resume. "You must tell your story quickly and effectively," she says. "A resume is simply a screening tool. Some jobs have as many as 100 applicants. It's unrealistic to think that any employer has all day just to sort through applications and resumes."

As employers eyeball your resume, they're scanning for specific information about you, the applicant. Among the qualities they're looking for are:

TRAINABILITY Does your resume show that you have started at the bottom and worked your way up? Busboy to waiter or bagger to cashier, an upward progression demonstrates that you can master tasks and be trained for added responsibilities.

SPECIFIC SKILLS Do you have the skills required to do the work expected in your new position? If you were successful selling encyclopedias door-to-door, then you may be able to sell home remodeling over the telephone.

KNOWLEDGE Can you demonstrate some specific knowledge that relates to the job you want? Do you want to be the political writer for the local newspaper? If so, it pays to know who's running for mayor.

RESPONSIBILITY Have you shown the employer that you can be trusted and relied upon? Even though you worked in a fast food restaurant and you're applying for a job at a bank, the fact that you handled the nightly cash receipts might impress the interviewer.

SUCCESS Can you demonstrate previous success? Did you double the number of subscribers on your paper route? Were you able to get referrals from satisfied customers after you painted their homes? Did you receive a bonus at your last job because you came up with a cost-cutting idea?

UNIQUE CONTRIBUTIONS Have you done anything special? Were you the Girl Scout who sold the most Girl Scout cookies in your town? Did you get your picture in the newspaper for a civic achievement?

All well and good, you say. That stuff sounds great—if you'd only ever held a job before! Your only experience may be that you mowed a few lawns, did some babysitting for the neighbors, were president of the Spanish Club, and played second-string guard on the basketball team.

Let's face it, at first blush, there doesn't seem to be that much to talk about.

"All first resumes start blank," observes Claire Carrison, a management consultant who operates the Millvale Executive Center in South Carolina. "But a little creative thinking can help identify some solid skills."

Carrison recommends taking a closer look at some of the skills you developed during your extracurricular activities and then "marketing" them to your prospective employer. "Let's take a look at the Spanish Club presidency," she says. "As president, you managed people, the other club officers and members. You spearheaded the candy sales drive that paid for the club members' trip to see a performance of *Carmen* at the Opera House. You managed a budget and did some simple accounting. Maybe you were responsible for developing a program so that your club meetings were interesting. You may have made presentations to the PTA or the faculty."

"The fact that you haven't worked for pay shouldn't be a problem," adds Carrison. "It just takes some practice identifying the skills you've acquired."

Once you've determined that you just might be employable, you should approach writing your resume with less foreboding.

Could You Put That in Writing, Please?

So what goes on your resume?

Now you begin the "making a list and checking it twice" mode. Both Carrison and Gardner suggest listing every specific task you've completed, stating how it positively contributed to the project or organization. In addition to your achievements in high school, list any current interest or extracurricular activities. If you've selected a major, note it.

If you've held jobs, related or otherwise, note these in the resume. If you had a title with that job, list it.

An employer recently reviewed the resume of a college graduate who listed his work history: manager of a men's clothing store. He had an interesting story to tell. When he was 16 years old, he started working at the clothing store, unloading merchandise in the basement. By the time he had graduated from college, he had worked his way up to managing the store during mid-week evenings. An impressive story. It got him the job.

Honors and awards, club memberships, campus activities, interests and hobbies, and military experience—or anything unusual—also belong on your resume. Skilled interviewers will often use your hobbies or interests as a basis for beginning an interview, to put you at ease and to see how you respond to general conversation. Including these hobbies in your resume makes their job easier . . . and you a more attractive prospect.

Let the employer know when you're available for employment. Can you start immediately? Monday? two weeks from now?

List references. References are people who know you, either through work or personally. Select those who will speak favorably on your behalf.

And get it all on one page. Remember what Gardner said,

most employers will spend less than half a minute looking at your resume.

Additionally, the University of Vermont Placement Manual recommends that you never use the word "I" in your resume. Also, use active verbs when describing your employment history and experiences.

Once you have the content of your resume, the format will be easy. Placement counselors at your school will help walk you through the resume-writing process. All resumes follow a basic style format: names, address, and telephone number on top, followed by a specific or general career objective, or position desired. Then you list all the previous jobs you've held, or, lacking work experience, the extracurriculars such as Spanish Club president. End with a brief mention of your personal interest. You may also include the stock line: References provided upon request.

Most first-time resume writers find it useful to model their resume after samples found on file in the counseling center or library. First and foremost, remember that employers are looking at content. But it's also imperative to have the resume look crisp, clean, and professional—devoid of typos or grammatical errors, or cutesy cartoons for visual aid.

On a final note, Gardner cautions every student about keeping his or her resume truthful. "Along with the TV commercial theme, I warn students about truth-in-advertising standards," she explains. "Be prepared; for any inherently false claims about yourself eventually will lead to your undoing."

Applying the Neat

Not all jobs require a resume. Instead, the employer may require that you complete an application. Here's the smart way to do it.

Take the application and have a couple of copies made. Carefully complete the information in longhand, making whatever corrections or changes are necessary. See how it reads. When you're satisfied, type that information onto the original application and return it to the employer.

Put yourself in the employer's shoes. She's looking at three applications. The first one is written in ink, and is very presentable . . . except for that huge coffee ring. The second is covered with erasures, misspellings, and is even lacking some of the requested information. The third is your typed application. Which resume is going to get her—positive—attention?

Placement counselors recommend that you also supplement the completed application with a resume—especially if your resume features the skills required for the position.

Job, Job, Wherefore Art Thou, Job?

You've written a great resume. And you know exactly what you're going to do when you're handed an application. All you need is to find a job.

Here are six paths to take to locate that job, the golden opportunity:

PLACEMENT OFFICE Turn first to your placement office, and get to know some of the counselors. Familiarity is never a disadvantage. If the counselor gets a call from an employer looking for the skills you just happen to have, you could find yourself at the right place at the right time. Beyond happenstance, the placement office walls and files are thick with opportunity. For the employer, it's a source that's hard to beat. Rather than run a newspaper advertisement and then deal with waves of applicants, many of whom will not meet the minimum requirements for the position, the employer can choose from a qualified pool of college students.

WORD OF MOUTH Referrals from family and friends are an oft overlooked source of job leads. Ask them if they know of anyone looking to hire a bright, hard-working college student (that's you.) A family friend once introduced me to the owners of a small food processing business who needed someone to paint their factory. It turned out to be a fabulous job.

NEWSPAPER ADS The local newspapers are filled with pages of "Help Wanted" advertisements. Don't forget alternative newspapers, or community newspapers, weeklies, or "throwaways." These other papers often offer jobs that aren't advertised in the major dailies. Comb these papers thoroughly. Your perfect job may be listed under some position you never considered before.

DOOR-TO-DOOR That's right, just "knock on the door" of any business and introduce yourself. Let the manager or owner know that you're looking for work. You'll be surprised at how favorable some of the responses to this approach will be. Most small business owners view themselves as entrepreneurs. They'll recognize in this tough, no-nonsense approach a shred of the determination they demonstrated when they began their business. If employers are sincere in wanting to hire self-starters, what could be better proof than just walking in and asking if there's any work available?

VOLUNTEERING Sometimes donating your time to a worthy cause will help introduce you to "the right people." If your commitment and hard work are recognized, they may not go unrewarded. A large donor, impressed by your efforts, could offer you a job.

CREATING A JOB On occasion, you may have an idea to improve a business, and in the process of selling that idea to the owner, you sell yourself. A student at the University of Vermont had been conducting a research project on the information systems on campus. When school officials realized that they needed to update the school's databases, they turned to the one individual who knew more about the programs than anyone else. The university hired the "kid."

Heed the Call

Once you've identified the job, you must respond to it. This means that you must contact the employer, by letter, by telephone, or in person. Some advertisements will ask that you respond by letter. A cover letter together with your resume is the best response. Don't be afraid to call a few days after responding by mail to ask if your letter was received. Follow-up is very important in landing a job. It also shows that you're thorough and conscientious.

Some employers will use telephone calls to screen applicants before inviting them in for a full interview. Prepare for this telephone call. A string of "uh's" will not inspire confidence. "Yeah, uh . . . like . . . uh . . . I sorta like saw this . . . uh . . . newspaper ad . . . uh . . . that like said you . . . uh . . . were looking for someone with . . . uh . . . good communications . . . uh . . . skills." Let's face it, you're nervous, and this is new ground you're covering. Write down what you intend to say . "This is Eloise Hanner, and I'm calling to inquire about the position you advertised in the *Sacramento Bee*. I believe that I'm qualified for the job. Is the position still available?" Which sounds better?

Provided you make the cut, you're now ready for your first trial by fire: The Interview.

We Have Ways of Making You Talk

"Between 40 and 50% of job applicants fail to establish eye contact," says Bob Beavers, Senior Vice President, Zone Manager for the Western U.S. for McDonald's Corporation. "Eye contact is the chief indicator of confidence."

McDonald's is the largest employer of youth in America, and Beavers has interviewed a good number of them during his 27-year career. "You must present yourself in the best possible light," Beavers counsels. "Give a good strong handshake, establish eye contact with the interviewer, and introduce yourself with confidence."

Beavers also recommends that you project a "flavor" of yourself. Tell the interviewer what extracurricular activities you enjoy, what your aspirations are, what you enjoy about school, and so on.

Another simple, but often overlooked detail, is how to dress for an interview. Wear clean, pressed clothes and make sure your

FAST SKILLS FROM FAST FOOD

Bob Beavers, Senior Vice President, Zone Manager for the Western U.S., McDonald's Corporation, says he's always impressed when applicants ask him what they should expect to get from a job. McDonald's turned out to be a lifetime career for him, but he thinks what he learned there could be applicable anywhere. "I think that a lot of kids first look at McDonald's as a way to make some quick cash, and don't realize what terrific skills they walk away with."

Claire Carrison, a management consultant who operates the Millvale Executive Center in South Carolina, also points out that skills can be transferred from one kind of job to another.

Here are some skills that you could develop while working in a fast food restaurant:

▼ Dealing with the public, customer service.

▼ Developing the ability to complete assigned tasks.

▼ Becoming an expert in one area—fries, for example. Sounds mundane, but nevertheless you will be an expert. And mastering one thing means you can master another.

▼ Becoming a teacher and a trainer. It won't be long before you'll be showing a new employee how to perform a specific task.

▼ Developing management skills; getting people to work for you.

▼ Punctuality

▼ Teamwork. The next time you're in a fast food restaurant, watch the activity behind the counter and in the food preparation area. That hamburger didn't make it to your tray by accident.

▼ Cooperation.

▼ Inquisitiveness. After you perfect one skill, you'll be eager to learn another.

hair is neat and clean. Don't walk into an interview in tattered jeans and smelling like you just came off the basketball court.

Prepare for your interview as diligently as you prepare for quizzes and tests in school. If you're trying to make a good impression, it's wise to do a little research on your potential employers. Ask publicly held companies to mail you annual and quarterly reports. Check the library's newspaper and magazine files for recent stories about the company. This is also a good way to investigate a privately owned business. If the business is a small one, call the local Chamber of Commerce. And if it's a "Mom and Pop" shop, the best way to check on the business is to walk in as a customer.

Be ready to talk about yourself, your goals and the skills you hope to acquire during your employment. Here's a good way to think about it: Can you talk about yourself for 20 minutes? To some that may sound easy; after all, you are your favorite subject. To others it will be terrifying. But try it. Chances are you'll be "uh-ing and ah-ing" in less than five minutes.

Walk into the interviewer's office, shake his hand, look him in the eye, and announce yourself.

And be ready to answer some questions:

"How would you describe yourself?"
"How would you describe the ideal job?"
"Why are you applying for this specific position?"
"How would your best friend describe you?"
"If I called your last employer, what would she say about you?"
"What do you consider your most significant accomplishment?"
"What are your strengths?"
"What is one area about yourself you'd like to improve?"
"What is your favorite subject in school?"
"Where do you see yourself in five years/ten years?"
"What have enjoyed most in your other jobs?"
"What did you dislike most in your last job?"
"What do you think it will take to become successful in this organization?"
"Do you get along with other people?"
"What do you like to do in your spare time?"

Here's more advice about interviews:

▼ *Be yourself.*

Answer the questions truthfully, but confidently. Don't try to give the interviewer the answers you think he wants. Good interviewers will ask the same question in different ways to ensure consistency.

▼ *Be prepared to ask questions.*

An interview is also a great opportunity to learn about the company and the people you'll be working with. If the interviewer offers you the opportunity to question him, then do it. Ask him how he got started in the company, or, if he's the owner, how he started the company. Ask the interviewer what he likes best about working for the company. By asking intelligent questions you'll further impress the interviewer.

▼ *Be ready for "Why?"*

Good interviewers ask open-ended questions that require answers beyond a simple yes or no. Be ready for "Why?" and "Give me an example of that." These follow-up questions afford you the opportunity to complete the picture of who you are and why you should be hired.

The Interns

Many universities offer intern programs for their students. The driving motivation is usually not money, but the opportunity to work in a chosen field, to see if you enjoy the work. If you've dreamed about working in a child-abuse clinic or special education program, it makes sense to seek out these experiences as an intern. Also, internships give you a head start and experience for positions you'll be competing for with other qualified graduates when it's time to get the "real" job.

Most intern positions are offered during the summer. Investment houses such as Merrill Lynch and Goldman Sachs offer positions for summer interns. Advertising firms, television stations, newspapers, public utility companies, government, and magazine publishers, all offer students the opportunity to spend a summer working for them. While some intern programs are done without any compensation (read that: you don't get paid!), others defray living expenses or offer a salary.

"A large number of internship programs, both summer and year-round, are offered to our students," says John Kupetz, Assistant Professor and Placement Director at Northwestern University's prestigious Medill School of Journalism. "Employers hope to get a serious-minded student with good basic writing skills. Our track record has been good. Most students find the internship a life-changing experience. It takes them from the world of academia to the real world."

"My newspaper internship had a tremendous impact on me," reports freelance writer Katherine Barrett, a graduate of NU's Medill School. "I never thought that I wanted to work for a daily newspaper, but I loved it. It's exciting to work on breaking stories and see your byline day after day. Editors reviewed my work every day, giving me feedback on everything from style to substance."

"One time I covered a public meeting, and I was shocked at the racist language being used. I went back to the office and couldn't stop talking about how these officials spoke, but then wrote the story on the purpose of the meeting. I never mentioned the racist remarks. My editor pulled me aside and told me the big story was the one I had left out. Boy, was he ever right!"

Barrett says she left her internship with a great deal of confidence and a clip book of articles she had written. "When I started to apply for full-time positions after graduation, I had a strong resume and samples of my work. It really put me head and shoulders over others competing for the same job."

Barrett ultimately left the dailies and is a contributing writer to *Financial World* and *The Ladies Home Journal*.

Internships can also help convince you that the profession you've dreamed about is not all that it's cracked up to be. You may find your experiences so unpalatable that you'd never spend another day working in that industry. A friend of mine took a summer internship at an advertising agency in New York City. He spent the summer at the copier and filling coffee pots, jobs he was convinced he would still be performing if he signed on full-time after he graduated. He took a position in personnel at a financial services company instead.

Internships can stoke the passionate fire, or dampen it. They can offer competitive salaries and living allowances, or you may work for nothing but the experience. But experience you will get.

The Negotiator

Unless you're interviewing for a minimum-wage job, there's usually a salary range. In addition to landing the job, you should endeavor to land the best salary. Management consultant Claire Carrison has some advice for you. "Find out about the salary range. During the interview you'll get some signals if the employer is interested in hiring you. The interviewer may say things like: 'How soon could you be available?' or 'I'd like you to meet some of the other people in the office...' or 'We're very interested.' Once you start getting these signals, you can expect to be offered a position."

Let's set the stage for a short drama. Cindy, our plucky coed, is interviewing for a job with Old Man Rivers. The salary range is $5.00 to $6.50 an hour. It may go a little like this:

OLD MAN RIVERS
Well, Cindy, I'd like to offer you a position starting at $5 an hour.

CINDY
Mr. Rivers, I'm really very glad to be offered this job, but I'd like to start at a higher level . . . $6 . . . which is still within the starting range you mentioned.

OLD MAN RIVERS
Honestly, Cindy, this is your first job and we'll be taking a big risk just hiring you.

(At this point the conversation could take a few twists and turns . . .)

CINDY
I don't honestly know if I can make ends meet on $5 an hour.

OLD MAN RIVERS

Uh . . well, I might be able to raise that to $5.50.

(*Hooray!* CINDY *got them to budge a little!*)

OR

OLD MAN RIVERS

We really can't justify a higher salary.

CINDY

Well, can I get a performance review in 60 to 90 days? If you're satisfied with my work would you then consider a raise of 50 cents an hour?

(*Here* OLD MAN RIVERS *may agree or adamantly refuse to hire* CINDY *at anything more than $5 a hour.* CINDY *must be prepared to accept the position or to tell* OLD MAN RIVERS *that she's sorry and can't accept the job.*)

This little negotiating drama also brings up another of Carrison's crucial observations. Once you've been hired, urge your employer to tell you exactly how your performance will be measured. Carrison has found that most companies don't have performance measurements. Your goal is to have your review be objective, not subjective. When you negotiate a salary increase, you'll be better equipped if you have met or exceeded your boss's stated expectations.

Here are some other points you might consider when you're weighing job offers. All of these may not be offered with a part-time position, but some may be very important.

HEALTH BENEFITS Medical and dental benefits may not seem important to you now, but it doesn't hurt to ask . . . especially if it's a hazardous job like feeding the lions at the zoo.

DISCOUNTS ON COMPANY PRODUCTS Retail clerks are usually offered 10-40% discounts on regularly priced merchandise at the shops where they work. This translates into an interesting fringe benefit. Depending on the job, you might also be offered free admissions, family discounts, or other money-saving benefits.

EDUCATION BENEFITS If you start working part-time and then become a full-time employee, you might find that some of your education will be paid for by the company. Education benefits are very common.

TIME OFF Know about this policy before you start. How much notice must you give your employer to get a day off, or to take a vacation? Most part-time positions are offered without vacation benefits.

Parting With Such Sweet Sorrow

When the summer internship ends, or that part-time job that helped you work your way through college gives way to your first "real" job opportunity, don't forget to ask for a reference. If you have been a good worker, your boss will take the time and write a "To Whom It May Concern"-type letter extolling your virtues as a loyal, hard-working, energetic self-starter ready to stride through the business world with giant steps. Employers may check job references when considering a candidate, and they weight the comments of these former employers very heavily.

So don't spend the last two weeks trying to "beat the system" by receiving maximum pay for minimum work. We all have a tendency to have a "short-timer's" attitude when we know we're leaving a job. Think of this as the spring fever of the employment world. But don't give in to it. You want to leave with the boss thinking he's lost the best employee he ever had and with you carrying a glowing letter of recommendation.

A MOST TAXING PROBLEM

▼ ▼ ▼

"... in this life nothing is certain but death and taxes."
BENJAMIN FRANKLIN, 1789

*When Al Capone, the famed 1920's Chicago gangster, was con-
victed and sentenced to 11 years in prison, it wasn't for bootleg-
ging, grand theft, murder, or any of the other lurid crimes he committed. There wasn't a daring car chase, a breathtaking machine
gun battle, or dogged police work. In fact, his arrest was surprisingly bloodless. You could go so far as to say that a No. 2 pencil
was Capone's undoing.*

▼

The man who put one of the century's most famous criminals in jail wasn't even a policeman. He was Treasury Department Special Agent Frank Wilson. The nearsighted, gun-shy Wilson coordinated a team of investigators. After conducting hundreds of interviews, examining bank records, and checking Western Union records, Wilson's investigators were able to prove that Scarface Al earned over $1,000,000 during the years 1924 through 1929, and had failed to pay his taxes. The most notorious and colorful criminal of the Roaring Twenties was arrested, tried, and convicted of tax evasion!

Ever since Congress first authorized a tax on income in 1894, there have been Americans who have tried to dodge the bullet. Not long ago, two well-known Americans, baseball batting star Pete Rose and real estate/hotel magnate Leona Helmsley, were investigated by the Internal Revenue Service for failing to pay their taxes. But not all tax evaders are celebrities. They include waiters, small business owners, doctors, at least one divinity student, and others. Their excuses come in all shapes and sizes: "Geez, I was too busy . . . for 14 years." Or, "The forms were too confusing. Besides, I was gonna get money back anyhow, so I wasn't really cheating." Or, "I don't approve of the way the government spends money, so I'm not paying a cent." There are even some die-hard tax evaders who claim that income taxation is illegal. The government willingly, and ruefully, admits that thousands of Americans fail to pay each year. The fact is, failing to pay taxes is illegal, and so is the failure to file.

Here we'll look at some of the things you need to know about taxes, specifically federal and state income taxes, Social Security taxes, sales tax, and "sin taxes." You'll receive tax tips and suggestions from tax professionals, as well as practical advice on how to reduce your taxes. You'll also be introduced to the 1040EZ, the tax form you'll most likely be completing during your first few years as a working adult. Adjusted gross income, W-2, 1099, exemptions, dependents—they're all defined here.

Oh, one final note on the divinity student. Although he had yet to be investigated by the IRS, he felt he needed to come clean, for he hadn't paid his taxes in years. He took advantage of a tax amnesty program which allowed people to pay their back taxes without fines or penalties. He said that he had to clear up his earthly obligations before he took his heavenly vows.

The First Paycheck: Before and After

Before . . .

Congratulations, you took the job! You now have to fill out a pile of forms that look very official and rather daunting. A Form W-4 will most certainly be included in that pile. This simple form accomplishes quite a bit: it establishes a tax file for you with the IRS, fulfills your employer's reporting obligation, verifies your Social Security number, and allows you to elect the number of exemptions you wish to take for tax purposes.

Your employer's payroll department uses the W-4 to figure how much in federal, state, and city income taxes to withhold from your paycheck. Some states have their own W-4 forms. The W-4 has a worksheet to help you determine the number of exemptions you may choose.

What's an exemption? Nobody has ever met one. But let's see if introducing another term, "dependent," can shed some light on exemptions. A dependent, in tax parlance, is a person who depends on you for basic care: food, shelter, and clothing. The number of exemptions you take usually corresponds to the number of dependents you have. If you're married and have five children, for example, you have six dependents, including your spouse. And you also "depend" on you, so you can claim seven exemptions by including yourself.

But some taxpayers choose to increase or decrease the number of exemptions they take, regardless of the number of their dependents. The more exemptions you claim, the less in taxes is withheld. How many exemptions should you claim? In most cases, the answer for the student is a simple "one."

"Generally, we don't recommend that students claim more than one exemption," counsels Judy Keisling, Assistant Vice President, Director of Tax Training of H & R Block, Inc. "Taking a large number of exemptions is short-term gratification. You'll get more money in each paycheck, more spending money, but it makes for one heck of a headache at tax time."

Keisling recommends taking either *no* exceptions or one exemption. "The choice is based on individual circumstances. By claiming zero the student will probably receive a tax refund. Some argue that by claiming one exemption you only get refund money that would be in your hands each payday for you to use as you see fit. The government doesn't pay interest on your excess payments. But many people *like* the forced savings. A tax refund check for $200 or $300 looks good . . . you can think of it as 'Uncle Sam's Christmas Club.'"

After . . .

Let's say the job you landed is at a local grocery store, which is paying you $5.50 an hour. You work 21 hours each week, and get paid every other week. You're looking forward to that fat paycheck. You figure you've worked 42 hours, so you've earned $231, and there's lots of places to spend that money. When the manager hands you the check, you rip open the envelope and . . . there must be some mistake! The total is only $184.25! How come?

First of all, the federal income tax is $27. Fortunately, you haven't made enough money for state income tax to be withheld; however, $2.08 is deducted for state disability insurance. Then there's FICA—Social Security withholding—and that comes to $17.67. Your total withholding comes to $46.75, slightly over 20% of your wages. That's a hefty bite.

By the way, this total doesn't include any voluntary payroll deductions you may have authorized. For example, you may have elected to have union dues deducted directly from your check . . . or enrolled in a voluntary savings program . . . or elected a group medical plan that requires a payroll deduction. So, your check might be a lot smaller.

Let's summarize these deductions briefly. First is the federal income tax withholding—your contribution to the federal coffers to help build roads, bridges, and Stealth bombers. Second is disability insurance—collected to provide a source of income for you should you become disabled and unable to work. Some states don't have disability insurance at all, some states have the employer pay, and others have you pay. Third, is FICA, or the Social Security tax—levied to pay for the Social Security benefits. This program was part of the New Deal, President Franklin D. Roosevelt's landmark social programs, and was originally designed to provide a "safety net" for retired workers with limited income. Finally, you may also have to pay state and local taxes—your way of helping to pay for police, fire, waste removal services, and schools.

The Taxman Cometh

In late January, your employer will mail you a Form W-2, Wage and Tax Statement, which summarizes your earnings for the previous year. The W-2 form will show the total income you received from your employer for that year, and also any taxes paid: federal, state, local, and FICA. The Form W-2 provides the basis for completing and filing your income tax return. *Don't* throw it away. You'll need it to file your taxes.

At about the same time, you'll also receive year-end statements from banks and other financial institutions that paid interest on your accounts, referred to as Form-1099INTs, and commonly called "10-99s." Interest is considered a form of income and it must be reported to the IRS. Once you've collected these forms and statements, you should have all the information you need to begin a rough draft of your taxes.

Getting sweaty palms and a nervous stomach? Do you need some help? Where do you go? If you're the do-it-yourself type, you can order Publication 4, "Student's Guide to Federal Income Tax." In fact, Publication 4 is a very handy guide to have around at tax time. The post office or library will have the address of the Forms Distribution Center that services your state. You can order Publication 4 and many other IRS forms and publications from that center.

In the meantime, here's some general information to help you get your bearings at tax time.

▼ *Does everybody have to file?*

Most everyone has to file, but there are some exceptions. First, you must determine if you're a dependent. Your parent or guardian can claim you as a dependent if he or she provides more than half your support for the year. Support includes any money spent for food, clothing, lodging, education, medical and dental care, recreation, transportation, and similar necessities.

If you are a dependent, then use this chart to determine whether you must file:

You must file a return if— your investment income was:	AND	the total of that income plus wages, tips, and other earned income was:
$1 or more		more than $500
$0		more than $3,100

▼ *What's investment income?*

Investment income is any interest you receive from savings or interest-bearing checking accounts or money-market funds. It would also include any dividends or interest you receive from stocks or bonds you own. If the income is derived as a result of an investment, it counts. Combine that with more than $500 in any earned income (money you've actually earned from your labors,) and you file. "Other earned income" includes any part of a taxable scholarship or fellowship grant.

▼ *What part of your scholarship is taxable?*

Some of your scholarship is taxable. The amount not used to cover tuition and fees required for enrollment or attendance, or for fees, books, supplies, and equipment required for your courses, is taxable. Specifically, the portion of the scholarship used to pay for room and board is taxable. If that scholarship is paid based on your providing services to the school, then that portion earmarked for those services is taxable.

▼ *Are students automatically considered dependents?*

A new rule states that full-time students over the age of 24 and earning over $3,000 can't be claimed as dependents. By law, rather than in fact, you're on your own. If you're not claimed as a dependent by anyone, then you must file an income tax return if your income for the year was $3,100 or more.

▼ *What if you're self-employed?*

If you're self-employed, the rules change. Your wages aren't reported on a Form W-2. Technically, all income earned from your labors—babysitting, mowing lawns, delivering newspapers, or cash payments for any job—is taxable. In fact, Publication 4 provides for a "self-employment" case using Schedule C, Profit or Loss From Business. These represent gray areas for income taxes. According to H & R Block's Keisling, "In theory, babysitting and mowing lawns result in taxable income. However, most students never report this income." Another gray area is tips. Waiters and waitresses face some income tax rules that single out the food-service industry. Waiters and waitresses are required to report their tip income to the restaurant. Federal, state, local, and Social Security taxes are withheld from this reported tip income.

CAUTION: Keep in mind that this book is not a substitute for the professional advice of a Certified Public Account, CPA. If you're in doubt about any tax matter, it's best to consult a tax professional.

Smiling and Filing

OK, it's time for another word problem. If a train leaves St. Louis and is traveling at 60 mph and another train . . . scratch that. Let's go back to our hardworking grocery-store employee, Gary, the one with the $231 bi-weekly earnings. Early in January, he receives his W-2 from his employer. This Form W-2 shows that Mab's Market has withheld $540 in federal income tax from total wages of $4,620. (The W-2 also shows that $353.40 of Social Security tax was withheld and that $41.60 was withheld for state disability insurance.) Meanwhile, Gary has also received a Form 1099INT, which shows he received interest of $76.85 from his money-market fund. He's also received a Form 1040EZ, complete with an instruction booklet, from the IRS. Our mission now is to help Gary fill out his Form 1040EZ, using the information he got from his W-2 and his 1099INT. To do this, we also need to know that Gary's parents will be claiming him as a dependent and that he isn't married. Ready? (See pages 121-122.)

Line 1 Fill in *total wages*(salary plus tips) from W-2 .... $4,620.00
Line 2 Fill in *interest income*from Form 1099INT 76.85
Line 3 Add lines 1 and 2 to get *adjusted gross income*........... 4,696.85
Line 4 Answer Yes—Gary's parents will claim him as a
      dependent. Fill in the *standard deduction* figured
      from the worksheet on the back of the
      form (page 122) 3,100.00

NOTE: If Gary's parents were not claiming him as a dependent, he'd answer No and fill in the standard deduction plus his *personal exemption.*

Line 5 Subtract line 4 (standard deduction) from line 3
      (adjusted gross income) to get *taxable income*......... 1,596.85
Line 6 Fill in Federal income tax already withheld (from
      Box 9 of W-2) 540.00
Line 7 Use the tax tables in the instruction booklet to
      look up the *tax due* on taxable income of
      $1.596.85 (line 5) 238.00
Line 8 Subtract line 7 (tax due) from line 6 (tax withheld)
      to get a *refund*.. 302.00

NOTE: If line 7 were larger than line 6—that is, if the tax due were more than the tax already withheld—you'd have to subtract line 6 from line 7 to get the *amount owed.*

Now all that's left is for Gary to fill in his address and Social Security number at the top (usually, the IRS provides a handy stick-on label for this purpose) and sign his name (and date) at the bottom. He can do this himself.

CAUTION: Don't forget to sign your name! Every year, thousands of people *do* forget . . . and get their forms returned to them. And, if you owe money, don't forget to include your check!

Department of the Treasury - Internal Revenue Service

Form
1040EZ

**Income Tax Return for
Single Filers With No Dependents** (5)   **1989**

OMB No. 1545-0675

**Name &
address**

Use the IRS mailing label. If you don't have one, please print.

L
A
B
E
L

Print your name above (first, initial, last)

H
E
R
E

Home address (number and street). (If you have a P.O. box, see back.)   Apt. no.

City, town or post office, state, and ZIP code

Please print your numbers like this:

9 8 7 6 5 4 3 2 1 0

Your social security number

☐☐☐ ☐☐ ☐☐☐☐

**Instructions are on the back. Also, see the Form 1040A/
1040EZ booklet, especially the checklist on page 14.**

Yes No

Presidential Election Campaign Fund
Do you want $1 to go to this fund?

*Note: Checking "Yes" will
not change your tax or
reduce your refund.* ▶

☐☐

Dollars | Cents

**Report
your
income**

1   Total wages, salaries, and tips. This should be shown in Box 10
of your W-2 form(s). (Attach your W-2 form(s).)   **1**

4 , 6 2 0 . 0 0

Attach
Copy B of
Form(s)
W-2 here.

2   Taxable interest income of $400 or less. If the total is more
than $400, you cannot use Form 1040EZ.   **2**

7 6 . 8 5

*Note: You
must check
Yes or No.*

3   Add line 1 and line 2. This is your **adjusted gross income.**   **3**

4 , 6 9 6 . 8 5

4   Can your parents (or someone else) claim you on their return?
☒ **Yes.** Do worksheet on back; enter amount from line E here.
☐ **No.** Enter 5,100. This is the total of your standard
deduction and personal exemption.   **4**

3 , 1 0 0 . 0 0

5   Subtract line 4 from line 3. If line 4 is larger than line 3,
enter 0. This is your **taxable income.**   **5**

1 , 5 9 6 . 8 5

**Figure
your
tax**

6   Enter your Federal income tax withheld from Box 9 of your
W-2 form(s).   **6**

5 4 0 . 0 0

7   **Tax.** Use the amount on **line 5** to look up your tax in the tax
table on pages 41-46 of the Form 1040A/1040EZ booklet. Use
the **single** column in the table. Enter the tax from the table on
this line.   **7**

2 3 8 . 0 0

**Refund
or
amount
you owe**

8   If line 6 is larger than line 7, subtract line 7 from line 6.
This is your **refund.**   **8**

3 0 2 . 0 0

Attach tax
payment here.

9   If line 7 is larger than line 6, subtract line 6 from line 7. This
is the **amount you owe.** Attach check or money order for
the full amount, payable to "Internal Revenue Service."   **9**

☐☐☐ . ☐☐

**Sign
your
return**

(Keep a copy
of this form
for your
records.)

I have read this return. Under penalties of perjury, I declare
that to the best of my knowledge and belief, the return is true,
correct, and complete.

Your signature   Date

X

For IRS Use Only—Please
do not write in boxes below.

☐☐☐☐

☐☐☐☐

For Privacy Act and Paperwork Reduction Act Notice, see page 3 in the booklet.   Form 1040EZ (1989)

1989   Instructions for Form 1040EZ

Use this form if:	• Your filing status is single. • You were under 65 and not blind at the end of 1989. • You do not claim any dependents. • Your taxable income (line 5) is less than $50,000. • You had **only** wages, salaries, tips, and taxable scholarships or fellowships, and your taxable interest income was $400 or less. *Caution: If you earned tips (including allocated tips) that are not included in Box 14 of your W-2, you may not be able to use Form 1040EZ. See page 23 in the booklet.* If you are not sure about your filing status or dependents, see pages 15 through 20 in the booklet. If you can't use this form, see pages 11 through 13 in the booklet for which form to use.
Completing your return	Please print your numbers inside the boxes. Do not type your numbers. Do not use dollar signs. You may round off cents to whole dollars. To do so, drop amounts under 50 cents and increase amounts that are 50 cents or more. For example, $129.49 becomes $129 and $129.50 becomes $130. If you round off, do so for all amounts. But if you have to add two or more amounts to figure the amount to enter on a line, include cents when adding and round off only the total.
Name & address	Please use the mailing label we sent you. It can help speed your refund. After you complete your return, put the label in the name and address area. Cross out any errors. Print the right information on the label (including apartment number). **If you don't have a label,** print your name, address, and social security number. If your post office does not deliver mail to your home and you have a P.O. box, show your P.O. box number instead of your home address.
Presidential campaign fund	Congress set up this fund to help pay for Presidential election costs. If you want $1 of your tax to go to this fund, check the "Yes" box. If you check "Yes," your tax or refund will not change.
Report your income	**Line 1.** If you don't get your W-2 by February 15, contact your local IRS office. You must still report your wages, salaries, and tips even if you don't get a W-2 from your employer. Students, if you received a scholarship or fellowship, see page 23 in the booklet. **Line 2.** Banks, savings and loans, credit unions, etc., should send you a Form 1099-INT showing the amount of taxable interest paid to you. You must report all your taxable interest even if you don't get a Form 1099-INT. If you had tax-exempt interest, such as on municipal bonds, write "TEI" in the space to the left of line 2. After "TEI," show the amount of your tax-exempt interest. **Do not** add tax-exempt interest in the total on line 2. **Line 4. If you checked "Yes"** because someone can claim you as a dependent, fill in this worksheet to figure the amount to enter on line 4.
	Standard deduction worksheet for dependents who checked "Yes" on line 4 A. Enter the amount from line 1 on front. A. ___*4,620*___ B. Minimum amount. B. ___500.00___ C. **Compare** the amounts on lines A and B above. Enter the LARGER of the two amounts here. C. ___*4,620*___ D. Maximum amount. D. ___3,100.00___ E. **Compare** the amounts on lines C and D above. Enter the SMALLER of the two amounts here and on line 4 on front. E. ___*3,100*___ **If you checked "No"** because no one can claim you as a dependent, enter 5,100 on line 4. This is the total of your standard deduction (3,100) and personal exemption (2,000).
Figure your tax	**Line 6.** If you received a Form 1099-INT showing income tax withheld (backup withholding), include the amount in the total on line 6. To the left of line 6, write "Form 1099." If you had two or more employers and had total wages of over $48,000, see page 35 in the booklet. If you want IRS to figure your tax, skip lines 7 through 9. Then sign and date your return. If you paid too much tax, we will send you a refund. If you didn't pay enough tax, we will send you a bill. We won't charge you interest or a late payment penalty if you pay within 30 days of the notice date or by April 16, 1990, whichever is later. If you want to figure your own tax, complete the rest of your return.
Amount you owe	**Line 9.** If you owe tax, attach your check or money order for the full amount. Write your social security number, daytime phone number, and "1989 Form 1040EZ" on your payment.
Sign your return	You must sign and date your return. If you pay someone to prepare your return, that person must sign it and show other information. See page 40 in the booklet.
Mailing your return	Mail your return by **April 16, 1990.** Use the envelope that came with your booklet. If you don't have that envelope, see page 49 in the booklet for the address.

How Not to Cook the Books

H & R Block's Judy Keisling offers this advice: "Students should get into the habit of filing their returns on time, even if they'll only receive a small refund. Some kids feel it's not worth the trouble. Wrong! Just file! Besides, it's illegal if you don't file."

Also in the vein of developing good habits, Keisling recommends that you begin saving certain types of receipts. You should start keeping records on medical expenses, interest and taxes paid, and other deductible items. Your charitable contributions or tithes require substantial documentation. Did you have a casualty loss—property stolen or damaged that wasn't covered by insurance—during the year? These may be dollar-saving deductions for you if you can prove them.

Keeping good records is especially important for those who are self-employed and must maintain accurate accounts of income and business-related expenses. If you have a summer job as a housepainter, for instance, you should show invoices for your income. Expenses might include brushes, thinner, paint, drop-cloths, and equipment rental or servicing.

If you're a waiter or waitress, Keisling also suggests that you keep a log of your tip income.

According to J. Stephen Hawkins, a CPA, some of the most common deductions are those associated with a job-related move. "It is critical that the taxpayer keep accurate records of this move," suggests Hawkins. First of all, the move must pass the IRS rules: it must be job-related and require that you move more than 35 miles from your current residence. "If so, all direct moving expenses can be deducted," continues Hawkins. "These include moving-van expense, mileage on your personal vehicle, airfare, 30-days' temporary living expenses up to $1,500, and meals." You'll probably face this situation after you graduate from college and land that first "real" job.

Thorough record-keeping can save you lots of time. And if you're ever audited, it can save you money.

Other Taxing Tidbits

Long before you learned about income tax and Social Security tax, you dealt with other taxes.

Sales tax is charged on most purchases in most states. Some states do not charge sales tax, and some states do not charge it on certain purchases—food and clothing, for example. New York charges sales tax on clothing items, while New Jersey—which considers clothing a necessity—does not. New Yorkers can be found haunting New Jersey shopping malls saving moving money: that $299 wool overcoat at Macy's in New York City costs over $24 more than the same coat in a New Jersey Macy's. Find out what the sales tax is when you go away to school, or relocate for that new job.

Then there are the "sin taxes," taxes on beer, wine, liquor, and cigarettes. User taxes, or "consumer" taxes can be found on other items such as gasoline. You'll also pay excise taxes for your car.

When it comes time to purchase that first condominium, townhouse, or house, you'll have to deal with property taxes. These taxes pay for services such as schools, roads, police and fire departments.

Taxes are inevitable. Taxes are part of everyday life. For the cities, states, and the U.S. Treasury that levy these taxes, they represent the revenues necessary to provide the services we demand as a society. Taxes don't have to be mysterious; they don't have to be a hassle. Keep your records straight, file on time, and make so much money that have to hire a crackerjack accountant to worry about it for you!

SCAMS AND GAMBLING

▼ ▼ ▼

"Please, take this free book," the well-dressed young man called to
me as I walked toward my gate at the airport. A voracious reader,
I couldn't pass up a free book, so I grabbed a copy of the book and
began to make my way down the corridor. But before I turned the
corner, the friendly bookmonger buttonholed me again. The book
was free, he insisted, but a "donation" might be in order. When I
asked if $5 would suffice, I was met with a beatific grin and the
assertion that this was "most generous." I handed the young man
a $20 bill, and he began to make change. He handed me a $5 bill
and said, "That's $5 for the book and $5 makes $10 and...." Then
he began to hand me another $5 bill. "Oh, my!" he gasped, gen-

uinely perplexed, "that's my last five. Tell you what. Give me the other $5 back and I'll give you a ten." Which I did. "And $10 makes $20. Thank you," he said, and disappeared into the crowd.

A moment later I realized that this sincere, well-dressed young man had given me only $10 back. I had been taken for $5. Even worse, when I looked closely at the book, I discovered it was just a standard Hare Krishna tract. I was so embarrassed that I rented a coin-operated locker, put the book into it, and walked off. I never claimed the book.

I grew up an inner-city kid, straight off the streets of Chicago. Loaded with street smarts, I was sure I knew every con and scam in the book. You'd never catch me falling for the old shell game or three-card Monte. But all it took was one well-scrubbed con artist's shortchanging me to prove that you can never know enough about how not to be taken.

Confidence men, or con artists, need victims. And one of their favorite targets just happens to be the young...you. There are a number of reasons that you look so good to them. For starters, if you're away at school, your "network" of family and friends—who would help you think about what you're getting into—is absent. Second, the con artist knows you're taking your first steps of independence. And he knows you're still inexperienced in the ways of the world, but eager to show that you know your way around. Third, strangers in a strange city are most vulnerable to the "kindness" of other strangers. Ask yourself why you should be so lucky to reap the rewards this stranger offers. Finally, you haven't done it all, seen it all, or heard it all, but you want it all. Con artists rely on this eagerness to draw you into the scam.

How can you make yourself scam-proof . . . well, almost scam-proof? Here's a crash course in street smarts.

The Pyramid

The "standard" pyramid scheme is a common scam that pulls in new victims each year. At the apex is the con man. To build his pyramid he must draw in others to provide him with a base of support. For example, he makes an irresistible offer to five new friends to be part of his "great deal." They, in turn, each "invite" five other friends to share in the great deal. Already the scam has roped in 30 people—5+25=30. If the 25 friends of friends each bring in 5 more, add another 125 to the list. Without this ever-expanding base, the pyramid cannot be supported, and eventually collapses. But it's not hard to see how quickly cash can accumulate when money is involved. And how tempting it might be to play—at first.

"Last year's scam was a pyramid scheme called 'Airplanes,'" explains Lieutenant Mark Shaw, Campus Police, Louisiana State University. "Students were asked to buy a ticket for $10 on an imaginary airplane. You bought this ticket from a fellow student. You were asked to attend a meeting and there you were told about this great game. By recruiting other students to buy tickets you could move up through the tiers of the airplane. You started in 'coach,' then worked your way up to 'tourist,' 'first class,' 'crew,' 'navigator,' 'copilot,' and finally to 'pilot.' The more folks you brought in, the higher up the pecking order you got."

And everyone wanted to be the pilot. Because at these meetings the airplane "landed" and the pilot could sell his airplane and cash out.

The pilot was usually paid off by some nondescript fellow in the audience. The pilot would enthusiastically wave his $250 in the air. What could be better? You pay $10 for your seat on the airplane and get to take $250 when the plane you pilot "lands."

Airplanes were landing all over LSU last year. At first the tickets were inexpensive, $10 or so, but soon the price got higher. Soon seats on these airplanes were $20, then $50, and finally $200. Certainly, some students were making money and others saw the promise of big money just around the corner. Just think about it, hundreds of students selling tickets to other students and doing all the work, recruiting new passengers, selling the tickets, and publicizing the meetings. This Airplane stuff seemed great, and appeared to be a never-ending opportunity.

Until the airplane crashed, that is. And the nondescript, anonymous fellow in the audience took off with all the money.

"And I do mean *all* the money!" exclaimed Shaw. "Not only was the con man skimming half the money from the ticket sales, but when a bunch of planes were ready to land, and the ticket prices were at a very high price, he just took off. No happy pilots, no more airplanes. Just a bunch of students who were a lot poorer."

Any type of chain letter, whether for money or gifts, works on the same principle. Continuous hordes of new victims are needed to build the ever-expanding base. And only those at the top of the pyramid continue to make the money.

What can you do about a scheme like this? "Just one thing," offers Mark Shaw. "Don't play. You can't win . . . and neither can your friends."

The Magazine Is in the Mail

Campus police chiefs and officers around the country report that one of the most prevalent problems they see is magazine subscriptions. Sometimes kids are pressured into buying magazines for more than they can really afford. Other times they pay for magazines they never receive.

"Kids are often intimidated by the strong-arm tactics of the magazine subscription salespeople on campus," says Lieutenant Eddie Rivas at the University of Nevada at Las Vegas. "Salespeople will force their way into the student's room and really put on the pressure. Sometimes the kids buy the magazines because they're scared and they just want these characters to clear out. And sometimes they end up spending more money than they can really afford."

At LSU, it isn't always a question of the magazine salespeople's being a bit aggressive. Often, it's a question of being downright dishonest.

"Our kids never even get the magazines they paid for," notes

Lt. Shaw. "Often the salespeople work for a subcontractor who is out of business shortly after his crew has hit the campus. Sometimes students will receive one or two copies of the magazine. When they inquire later, the voice on the other end of the line informs them that the subscription was never actually paid."

Later, when students call the telephone number of the magazine subscription subcontractor, they find that the number is no longer in service. Usually, this unscrupulous subcontractor has opened up shop under another name and is continuing with this scam.

A detail that makes this such a easy scam is that the salespeople are always college-age kids, ostensibly "working their way through school."

"Another problem occurs when they're signing these kids up for the magazines. They'll say something like 'I bet you like car racing' or 'You look like you enjoy *Cosmo*' and before you know it they are handing you an order form for two or three magazines. When the student protests, the salesperson says he thought they meant to buy the magazine and he can't tear up the order form. Being good kids, they then pay for two or three magazines."

Lt. Rivas warns of magazine subscription problems during a student orientation, where other common crimes against students are discussed. "Just beware of the hard sell," says Lt. Rivas. "Most solicitors on campus shouldn't be there, so look upon them with skepticism. If it's too good to be true, it probably is."

Campus Fagins

You're wise to the pros, you'd never fall for a con. But . . .

Sergeant Irvin Summers, a 20-year veteran of the campus police at the University of Illinois in Champaign, Illinois, considers theft to be one of the biggest problems students face.

"Students coming to the campus from the rural Midwest seldom lock the doors at home and sometimes leave car keys in their automobiles. They lived in small communities where everyone knew and trusted each other. They carry that trust to the campus."

"Students from Chicago and other larger cities are generally more cautious. But when they leave the city, they sometimes let their guards down."

"A theft takes only a few seconds. Students tell me that they just left their rooms for a Coke, or they just left their books at the library for a minute to do something else."

Why is theft such a problem on campus? First, students feel that the campus is a safe haven from real-world problems. Second, as a result of students' lax security, thieves see them as easy targets. Third, other students want what you have, and take it.

So, how do you hang on to what's yours? How do you reduce the chances of becoming a victim of theft?

In your dorm. Your best protection is locking the door to your room, even when you step out for a soda or use the bathroom. This also means locking the door at night, when you're asleep. Students wake up and often find items missing from their rooms.

In public places. There are places on campus where your personal items are at a higher risk, such as gyms, student unions, and the

THESE ARE A FEW OF MY FAVORITE THINGS...

What are the most popular items for campus thieves? Favorite items seem to be small electronic devices—radios, CD players, calculators, and Walkmans. But thefts are not restricted to luxury items. Wallets and purses, cash, clothing, backpacks, even books, are favorite targets. (Books? Since the price of some textbooks is often $40 or $50, it's not hard to see why it makes perverse economic sense to purloin a copy of the latest edition of *Principles of Economics.*) And that's not all. Campuses have also reported thefts of bomber jackets and even athletic shoes. Again, a pair of Nike Air Jordans or Reebok's The Pump can cost from $130 to $175, so it's not surprising that these items are attractive to thieves.

library. You think you're safe and you feel comfortable because there are several other people around. The thief relies on this false sense of security. Keep your personal items nearby, and keep an eye on them.

In the car. Every year, you hear the sad tale of a family without presents because someone stole the brightly wrapped packages from the car. You shouldn't leave items in plain view on the seats or the floor of your car. Cassette tapes, cameras, books, and packages make for tempting tidbits. And remember to lock your car doors at all times.

In general. Don't tempt a thief, and don't make it easy for him. There are people who make a living stealing from students. Don't be a target.

Scams du Jour

Campus police warn of other dangers waiting for you.

RELIGIOUS CULTS Religious cults continuously recruit new members. They prey on students with low self-esteem, or students who are feeling uncomfortable in making the transition from home life to campus life. At first, religious cults may seem to offer a sense of belonging. Skeptics say these groups are ultimately after your money. Is this a fair trade: your belongings for belonging?

COVER GIRL At the University of Illinois, a "professional photographer" preyed on women students. Professing to be looking for models, he would regale his victims with promises of big money, professional contracts, and magazine covers . . . if they'd just pay him a small sum. He often had coeds pose in the nude. The photos and the fame never came.

BAIT AND SWITCH Bait and switch is an old technique used by some retailers to encourage store traffic and raise sales. You see a CD player advertised for $59 at a stereo store and you rush out to buy it. When you get there, the saleswoman explains that the only one left is the floor demo and that she can't sell that one. (To satisfy the law, at least one unit of the advertised item must be available.) But she has others, even better, in fact, for $159 "right over here." Bait and switch is illegal, by the way. However, your only recourse may be to complain to the local Better Business Bureau.

THE "LOST/STOLEN WALLET" SCAM The lost or stolen wallet scam is very popular at freeway rest stops. Some forlorn-looking man or woman will come up to you and tell you the sad story about how their wallet's been stolen or is lost. They point to their car, filled with kids and luggage. Gee, all they need is a few bucks to be able to buy some gas and get home. They will ask for your name and address and promise to mail you a check when they get home. What makes this con work so well is that it appeals to the Good Samaritan in you. The story is so convincing. If you were in this situation, wouldn't you want someone to help you out? That's exactly what the confidence man is counting on. Many people offer a few dollars to help out the stranded traveler. Most of them are still waiting for that promised check.

Gambling

Gambling is another potential pitfall for students. Playing the ponies, card games, football pools, and the like are often viewed as part of growing up. They conjure images of camaraderie, good times, and a sense of excitement. Gambling seems harmless, at first, but the danger is losing more than you can afford to lose. What that means is the difference between losing a few bucks and losing two months' living allowance. If this sounds like an exaggeration, it's not.

At UNLV, the problem of gambling takes on even greater proportions. "Students lose their tuition money, or book money," reports Lt. Rivas. "With slot machines in every restaurant, even at the airport, the temptation is constant."

Keep in mind, gambling laws are different in each state. Technically, something as innocuous as the old 100-box football pool is illegal in some states. High-stakes floating craps games and poker games are not just the stuff of Hollywood; look hard enough and you can find them on many campuses.

Detective Neary's University: Pros and Cons

Pros

Meet Detective Pete Neary, a 24-year veteran of the Chicago Police Department. For 20 of those years, he has worked property crimes: crimes committed by pickpockets, confidence men, and thieves. Here's a short course in street survival from Dean Neary of The School of Hard Knocks.

"Pickpockets are real artists," says Neary. He once watched a pickpocket lift a wallet out of a pair of skin-tight jeans. The target was a policeman at a seminar; the former pickpocket was working with police helping them catch other pickpockets. "The copper said he never felt a thing!"

"Everyone watch out! There might be a pickpocket around here!" Imagine hearing that warning while you're waiting in line for a movie, or standing outside an art museum waiting for the doors to open, or watching for a train at a crowded subway platform. What's your first instinct? Right. You check your purse, or you pat your pocket where you keep your cash. The only problem is that this helpful warning was probably shouted out by a *jouster*—a pickpocket's partner. While you were checking your wallet, the pickpocket was checking you—he has marked the location of many wallets and pockets where cash is kept.

According to Neary, pickpockets often work in twos. The jouster is the set-up man, or woman. He bumps you, or pushes you, or creates a diversion which then allows the pickpocket to make his score.

Neary discussed a pair he was after recently. The team consisted of a very fat woman and a skinny man. Their favorite targets were businessmen and tourists at Chicago-area hotels. Together they would choose a target and follow him into an elevator. The woman, laden with shopping bags and parcels, would position herself in front of the target while her slender partner would insinuate himself behind him. She would press the button for a floor just before the target's; if he was getting off on 12, she would press 10 or 11. When the elevator stopped at her chosen floor she would bend down, thrusting ample buttocks into the target. The target would be pushed into the pickpocket who would have the wallet out in a flash.

Here are some other tricks pickpockets use. The jouster will thrust an arm or a foot into a closing elevator door. While you scramble to hold the door, the pickpocket (who is already in the elevator with you) helps himself to your wallet or purse. Another diversionary tactic is to clog up the entrance to an escalator or an elevator by dropping something. As the jouster bends down to pick up his belongings, the pickpocket is moving through the crowd lifting wallets. Favorite targets on escalators are women with backpacks.

How do you keep someone from picking your pocket? "Be alert, be aware, be tuned in," Neary says. He suggests that women carry shoulder bags with zippers and pull the strap over head and shoulder. Men should keep their money in a front pocket. Also, don't keep your wallet or purse in a backpack or fanny pack. It's hard to tell if someone behind you is unzipping your pack.

Cons

Even though some "confidence games" seem far-fetched, they still work because the victims are willing participants. "Confidence men are really slick," said Neary. "They're experts at playing on human weakness and greed. They rehearse their scams constantly. In the theater of the streets, the con man is an Academy Award winner."

Detective Neary warns about the "Pigeon Drop," a con that still works after hundreds of years. "Instead of being worked at town fairs or farmers' markets, this scam now is played out at bus stops or airports." Its premise is "you can't cheat an honest man."

The targets are generally college-age guys, who are more approachable than women, but still lacking in "street smarts." The crimes often go unreported because the target is embarrassed to have been "taken."

"Look what I found!" says the man sitting next to you at the bus station. He shows you an envelope filled with money. "Why there must be $10,000 in here!" he exclaims. Soon you are joined by a third man and the question of what to do with the money is hotly debated. The third man generally claims to work for an attorney. He makes a telephone call and asks for the attorney's opinion. The attorney will offer advice along these lines: if you hold the money for 30 days and it's not claimed, then it belongs to whoever found it. The attorney will offer to notify the proper authorities, but declines to hold the money. Instead, he suggests that you each put up earnest money, to be held by one of you. Another should hold the addresses and telephone numbers of the group, and they third gets to hold the envelope with the $10,000. It is decided that you all come up with $500 apiece. One guy will hold the $1500, one guy will hold the telephone numbers of everyone involved, and you get to hold the envelope with the $10,000. That's because you're a college kid and you seem so honest. You figure that this is the greatest thing that has happened to you in your entire life. If you don't have the money on hand, don't worry, the con men will drive you to your bank so that you can withdraw $500, usually your book or tuition money. Soon enough, you'll be splitting $10,000 with your new pals, and anyway you're holding the money. After you hand over the $500, you are given the envelope and your threesome breaks up. When you get home, you open the packet— and discover that you are no longer holding an envelope filled with twenties. Instead, you have a packet with a single $20 bill and about fifty $1 bills. Somewhere along the line, envelopes were switched. Obviously, you never hear from your friends again.

Another scam involves "counterfeit money." This miniature drama is normally played out in front of a supermarket. The targets are often young shoppers. The con man watches as you pay for your purchase with a twenty dollar bill. When you leave the store, he will flash a badge and claim to be a police officer. He'll tell you he has reason to believe that the $20 you just used in your purchase is counterfeit and he would like to see the rest of your money. He may ask where you got the money and then mention that your particular bank or ATM has been identified as the source of these counterfeit bills.

"Sure enough, some or all your remaining $20's are counterfeit and he must confiscate this 'funny money,'" says Neary. "He will give you a receipt to bring to a local law enforcement office so that your money can be replaced. When you go to the police station and present your receipt, you're told that you've been taken."

Variations of this scam have cost victims thousands. Two con men, posing as Treasury agents, FBI, or policemen, will enlist the aid of a good citizen in stopping a counterfeiting operation. They ask the citizen to go to his bank and withdraw the entire amount in his checking or savings accounts in cash. These bogus law enforcement types have actually been known to drive the victim to the bank and home again.

"Just remember that no law enforcement agency will do this," says Neary. "Stop a minute and think about it. Someone flashes a badge and then writes you out a receipt for the money you hand over. Sure, it may sound plausible. Sure, you may think you're doing a civic duty. And, sure enough, you can kiss that money goodbye."

Neary says that confidence men pick out their victims and he offers some advice on how to beat them. "If you look like a wide-eyed tourist in the Big City, you're a prime target." Neary suggests that you don't wear clothing that identifies you as an out-of-towner, "An 'I love Seattle' tee-shirt worn in downtown Chicago marks you for the criminal." Neary also suggests that you learn your way around your new town. Don't become a victim because you got off at the wrong bus or subway stop. If you think that someone's a thief or pickpocket or con man, Neary offers the following advice: "Stare at him. These guys rely on being just another face. If you look at them hard, it makes them uncomfortable and they split."

The Right to Say No

By now you're probably feeling like last honest person on Earth. The intention is not to paint a bleak picture, but rather, a realistic one. You've spent your life trusting people—your parents, family, friends, and teachers. Hopefully, adults and authority figures have treated you with respect. You have been asked to believe in many things, to put your faith in what you've been told. The scamster, the confidence man, the thief, all rely on that trust and faith.

As LSU's Lt. Shaw says, "You have the right to say no. If something seems peculiar or strange to you, then trust your judgment. Don't mistake the appearance of sincerity as the genuine article. The college experience is as much about judging people as it is about anything."

"No" is as easy to say as "yes." You want to be a nice guy, you don't want to hurt another person's feelings, and it may not be in your nature to mistrust someone, especially someone in apparent need. So maybe you will say yes, and find yourself a victim. If you are, then learn from it. If you get scammed by a con man, ask yourself, what did I fall for? If you're the victim of a pickpocket, ask yourself, how was I careless?

Figure out what you did wrong, and become a bit wiser for the experience.

INSURANCE 101:
INSURING YOUR STUFF

▼ ▼ ▼

My first close encounter with insurance came when I was in elementary school. Student insurance, offered by a daily newspaper for a mere pittance, paid the policyholder for various and sundry dismemberments. If, for example, you lost an eye, the insurance company would pay you $500. An arm was $750. If you lost your leg, you hit the jackpot of $1,000. The money looked mighty big to a fourth-grader. During recess, Joey, Louie, and I would sit around and figure out different permutations and the expected payout. "Wow! If I lose an eye and a leg," mused Joey, "I'll get $1,500!" I guess we figured we had a spare of each.

nsurance has been the subject of jokes for many generations, perhaps rightfully so. Insurance is, after all, a bet you don't want to win. No one likes to think about it, and no one likes to pay for it, but everyone has to take insurance seriously.

Two types of insurance that students typically purchase are automobile insurance and renter's insurance. What kind of coverage do you need? Why does car insurance for college-age drivers cost about as much as the arm and the leg the fourth-graders were willing to cash in? What happens if your waterbed explodes and shorts out the stereo?

Here's a road map through the jargon that sometimes makes insurance harder to understand than it really is.

Drive Into the Danger Zone

Your first encounter with insurance will probably be insuring the student chariot. More than likely, you'll be included as a "permissive driver" on your parents' policy. This means you have permission to use the car and that the insurance company agrees to cover you—for a price that may be hefty. You'll know when this happens because your father will begin to have apoplectic fits upon opening the bill from the insurance company. Most insurance companies allow you to be carried on your parents' policy while you're in school, generally up to age 25. However, if the car is registered in your name, you have to get your own car insurance.

How insurance companies determine rates has bewildered generations of policyholders. Insurance companies set rates for different types of coverage based purely on statistics, and those statistics are derived from a wide range of factors. Let's look at a few.

The Who

AGE Sad, but true, the age of a driver is the single most reliable indicator of accidents and losses. The younger the driver, the more likely he is to have an accident. A young driver is 2 to 3 times more likely to have an accident than an older driver.

GENDER "He" was deliberately used above because "he" is more likely than "she" to have an accident. Young men are 4 times more likely to be involved in an accident than young women.

MARITAL STATUS Wedding vows and rings generally lower the cost of insurance. Married drivers statistically have fewer accidents than unmarried drivers of the same age. In fact, some insurance companies consider married females, no matter how young, as adults, thereby qualifying for a lower rate. On the other hand, unmarried men might not be classified as adults until age 49! Boys will be boys.

The What

PRICE Generally, the more the car costs, the more you'll have to pay for insurance. A Jaguar costs more to insure than a Nissan Sentra. If the car is stolen, the more expensive car will cost the insurer more to replace.

REPAIR On the heels of "price," parts for an imported Jaguar run substantially higher than comparable parts for a car from the "Big Three"—General Motors, Ford, and Chrysler.

AGE The older the car, the cheaper it is to insure, unless you're tooling around in a genuine classic, like a 1965 Corvette.

SAFETY RECORD Plain and simple, some cars are just safer than others. The better the safety record, the less you pay for insurance.

The Where

URBAN VS. RURAL Driving in New York City is more dangerous to your car's health than driving in rural Ohio. In fact, driving in some cities is more hazardous than driving in others. Some states are more expensive than others. Rates in California and New Jersey run higher than those in Montana or Wyoming.

PHYSICAL ENVIRONMENT Where you keep your car and where you drive can be big factors in insurance costs. Is the car garaged or parked on the street at night? How far is your commute, and are you heading into a densely populated urban area? Are the drivers in your region more prone to lawsuits? Even climate is a factor. Cars driven in the severe winters of the Midwest through sleet and snow—and the salt and sand laid on the roads to combat the elements—tend to depreciate faster. You rarely see this type of rust damage in the Sunbelt (where faded paint can be a problem, however.) All this falls under "territorial rating."

Statistics is simply information that's been collected, organized and interpreted. It enables insurance companies to analyze a particular segment of the population. For example, one source of information is the California Highway Patrol. Statistics released by the CHP for 1988 showed that 28.9% of the licensed drivers in California were under the age of 30, yet they accounted for 45.2% of all drivers in fatal and injury accidents.

How do insurance companies use these statistics? Greg Rossiter, a spokesman for Allstate Insurance Company, highlights the usefulness of statistics. "We see a greater percentage of accidents in 'muscle cars' versus 4-door sedans," he says. "That means we charge more for insuring a muscle car. The difference in rates between a Chevrolet Camaro and a Ford Tempo is +75%. That's a lot of money just to drive a flashy car."

Statistics are also kept on how often certain models are stolen. Some cars can be started with a screwdriver, others are wanted for spare parts.

Some cars are considered safer than others. The Insurance Institute for Highway Safety (IIHS) studied the 103 biggest selling 1985-87 cars and issued a list showing the 10 cars with the lowest death rates and the 10 with the highest. The Volvo 740/760 4-door topped the list with lowest death rate: 0.6 deaths per 10,000 autos registered. The Chevrolet Corvette came in with the highest death rate: 5.2 deaths per 10,000 cars registered.

The IIHS noted ". . . of the 10 cars with the lowest death rates, three are large and six are midsize cars. Only one is small. Twelve of the 15 cars with highest death rates are small, the other three are midsize. None is large."

You can use statistics to help lower your insurance bill. You could buy a safer, less expensive car. You could park your car in a secure garage. You could even get married! However, sometimes you're a victim of statistics. You can't help being a guy who's 19 years old and goes to school in LA.

Gobbledygook Explained

There are five categories of basic car insurance: liability, medical, collision, comprehensive, and uninsured motorist.

LIABILITY This is considered to be the most important coverage. Liability coverage protects you from claims for property damage and bodily injury that you cause in an accident. General minimums are $15,000 for one person, $30,000 for two or more persons, and $10,000 worth of property. Most states require that drivers have liability coverage.

MEDICAL Regardless of fault, all passengers in your car need to be covered. Medical coverage provides for hospitalization, physical therapy, and other medical procedures, should a passenger in your car be injured in an accident. Typical coverage ranges from $2,000 to $100,000.

COLLISION This covers your own vehicle in an accident. Let's say you're at fault in an accident. Your insurance company not only pays the claims against you, but also pays to repair your car.

COMPREHENSIVE This covers losses not related to a direct automobile accident. If your car is stolen, your Blaupunkt cassette deck ripped off, or Hurricane Hugo sent a cypress through the windshield, "comprehensive coverage" provides for payment.

"BRILLIANT DEDUCTION, HOLMES!"

With comprehensive coverage, as with collision, a "deductible" is used. Simply put, this means you end up paying a portion of the total cost of the replacement or repair.

Let's use an example. You've selected comprehensive coverage with a $250 deductible. While driving down the highway, a rock hits your windshield and shatters it. Nobody's fault, it just happened. You file a claim with your insurance company and get the windshield replaced for $348.67. You pay the deductible of $250, and your insurance company pays the remaining $98.67.

UNINSURED MOTORIST Not everyone driving a car has insurance, or even a license, for that matter. Even though it's against the law in 42 states, people have been known to climb behind the wheel of an automobile without insurance. They also get into accidents. Uninsured motorist coverage provides for this occurrence. If you are hurt or your car is damaged in an accident where the other party is at fault and uninsured, then your only recourse may be through your own insurance company. The same minimums as liability coverage apply here: $10,000 for property damage, $15,000 for one person, and $30,000 for two people in bodily injury coverage.

The best way to learn about the five types of coverage is through the experiences of my friend Micki. She learned them while on the phone with her insurance company the morning after the accident.

On her way to a meeting, Micki did some last-minute grooming in the car. While looking into the rearview mirror to apply her lipstick, she rear-ended a truck stopped at a red light. She wasn't wearing a seat belt, a fact that became painfully obvious to her as her head crashed into the windshield—but she was able to walk away, albeit a bit groggy, from the accident. Her car was nearly "totaled"—a total write-off for the insurance company. This means it's cheaper to replace than fix what's left of the car after an accident. There was some damage to the truck, but the driver was not hurt.

When the police arrived, they first made sure that everyone was okay. Then the policeman asked Micki for her license . . . which had expired . . . several years before. A passerby had called for an ambulance, and while Micki was being helped into it she watched her car being hooked up to the tow truck. To add insult to injury, the policeman handed her three citations: one for reckless driving, one for driving without a seatbelt, and one for failing to have a valid driver's license.

Because Micki was responsible for the accident, she was "liable" for the damage to the other vehicle.

Micki was fortunate that she hit a truck; the damage was minor—a dented fender. Because the truck driver wasn't hurt, she wasn't liable for any bodily injury.

In terms of medical coverage, Micki was again fortunate. She was driving alone. Her own medical bills, including paying the city for the ambulance, were covered. Her injuries were minor, and there was no damage to that Cover Girl look.

But here's where Micki's luck ran out. Her car was totaled. The insurance company issued a check for the value of her Honda Prelude, less the $1,000 deductible. The check Micki received was hard-earned through extensive negotiations. The company originally offered $5,200, and she ultimately received $9,800.

It's tempting to get just the minimum coverage for liability insurance. After all, logic would dictate that as a student you aren't particularly wealthy—even if you're sued, you can't pay anything, so who cares? You should care. If you're involved in an accident where someone is killed, crippled for life, or seriously injured, a jury can make the at-fault party pay for life. (Drunk drivers, or people driving under the influence of a drug, are treated most severely in these instances.)

Increased liability coverage doesn't cost you an arm and a leg either. In fact, it's one of the "bargains" in your overall policy. Many insurance agents advise that you insure yourself well above the minimum.

One place to save money on your insurance is by raising the deductible for comprehensive or collision. If you are driving a $350 jalopy, why even bother to have this kind of coverage? The cost of repairs almost ensures that even a steep deductible, $250-$750, will be reached. The higher the deductible, the lower your costs in these two categories.

You can also decide to be one of the uninsured motorists. This is just plain stupid. Most states require drivers to carry proof of insurance in their cars, along with vehicle registration. If you are stopped by a policeman and cited, the fine alone can run hundreds of dollars. Get into an accident and you will face lawsuits—against you personally. In either case, your license will be suspended until you can prove that you do have insurance coverage.

About half the states mandate no-fault insurance. No-fault insurance does away with the concept of determining fault in an accident. In other words, it doesn't matter who is at fault. Your insurance company pays for your claims, and their insurance company pays for their claims. No-fault eliminates lawsuits and guarantees immediate payment for injuries. Critics of no-fault, mostly those in the legal field, claim that it doesn't compensate fairly for injuries.

You Play, You Pay

So, you're convinced that it's smart to get car insurance. While this insurance may be expensive, there are ways to reduce the cost. Being a careful driver can pay off even if you're a young driver. Most insurance companies offer good drivers preferred rates. The definition of a good driver? No accidents, claims, or tickets. The definition of preferred rates? You pay less money.

In fact, being a good student also may mean less money shelled out for insurance. Allstate's Rossiter says, "We offer a student discount if your grades are a B average or better. This 15% discount is offered to these students because statistically students with better grades are better risks. I didn't say better drivers, just better risks."

Be aware of other discounts available for car owners. Airbags, anti-lock brakes, and anti-theft devices also help reduce the cost of insurance. (And here's a tip for later in life. Insure your life, home, boat, art collection, spouse—well, you get the message—with the same company. As a rule, the more you insure, the better the insurance rates will be.)

A traffic ticket or accident really affects your record, and translates to higher costs for at least a couple of years. Parking tickets won't get you into hot water with your insurance company, but moving violations such as reckless driving, running a red light or stop sign, speeding, tailgating, etc., will result in higher insurance rates.

Then there's DUI or DWI, the BIG one. Driving Under the Influence or Driving While Intoxicated will ensure that your life will be miserable. Penalties for drunken driving (or driving while under the influence of any other drug) are very stiff. In many states you will lose your license, plain and simple. You could spend time in prison or be sentenced to enter a rehabilitation program. Some insurance companies will drop you immediately. In the best case, you're going to end up in the highest risk pool that you can be assigned to by your insurance carrier.

The cost of your peccadillos? A speeding ticket on an otherwise clean record can result in a 20%-50% increase in your insurance costs. DUI is much worse. When I called my insurance company to give them a hypothetical case, I was told that in my case my coverage would increase 398% and that I would remain in that risk pool for three years!

The designated driver idea suddenly makes even more sense, doesn't it?

Renter's Insurance

Exactly what is renter's insurance? Renter's insurance covers your possessions against theft or damage, and also provides liability coverage against injuries and damage that occur in your apartment or rented home. If you're living in a dorm or chapter house for a fraternity or sorority, then you probably won't need renter's insurance.

You might not need renter's insurance even if you have your own place. You're probably covered under your parents' homeowner's coverage. Generally, a homeowner's policy will insure up to 10% of the property covered away from the primary residence. Old furniture, clothes, etc., in a storage facility would be covered, for example. This coverage also applies to your property while you're at school. If the value of your property exceeds 10% of the total household goods covered under your parents' policy, then it makes sense to get the coverage.

If you decide to get a renter's policy, what type of coverage should you get? You will need liability coverage. This will protect you against any claims made against you if someone is hurt while in your apartment. Liability coverage will also be handy if you burn down the place during a wild party or your waterbed suddenly finds its way from your second-floor apartment to the first floor.

Renter's insurance will also cover against loss or damage to your personal property. Ask specifically if the policy pays under a *cash value* clause or a *replacement value* clause. Cash value allows the insurance company to depreciate your property. In other words, the value of the property diminishes with age and use. Let's say you have a stereo system that you received as a graduation present. It's a top-of-the-line system and cost $1,400 new. Three years later it's stolen and the insurance company is ready to pay. A new system would now cost $2,000; however, after depreciation the stolen system is valued at $650. That's what you'd get under a cash value clause. Under a replacement value clause, you'd get $2,000, so you could actually replace the stolen stereo system.

As with automobile insurance, there is a deductible for renter's insurance. If your deductible is $200, then the check to replace the stolen stereo system in the example above would be $1,800.

Read the policy over very carefully. You will find that most insurance companies set limits on specific items. An insurance company may replace only $200 in cash, or $1,000 in jewelry. If you own an extensive stamp, coin, or baseball card collection, ask about an insurance "rider." This special amendment to your policy allows you to specify a particular item to be insured. It will cost you a bit extra but it helps safeguard your collection. Also be sure that you ask about your computer. If a computer is used for business purposes, you will need a computer rider. Personal use of a computer (homework, videogames, etc.) will normally bring the machine under standard coverage.

Once you decide you need some insurance coverage, take a little time to shop around. Ask friends and family members which companies they work with and if they're happy. Compare rates. Ask for discounts. Resist sales pressure. Read and reread the policy to make sure you completely understand the terms and conditions of your coverage.

A last word on the subject of insurance. In your life you have bought, and will buy, lots of stuff: cars, houses, clothes, electronics, services from professionals, and a host of other items. You are also buying something when you take out insurance. "You are buying protection against loss," says Greg Rossiter. "You are really buying peace of mind."

IN SICKNESS AND
IN HEALTH

▼ ▼ ▼

*Hospital Point is the home of many intramural sports at the U.S.
Naval Academy in Annapolis, Maryland. But in the winter—when
the ground is as hard and unforgiving as cement—fieldball is
king. It's not just a game, fieldball is a game with a purpose . . .
which appears to be to provide fodder for the operating tables of
resident orthopedic surgeons.*

*The object of the game is to score goals by firing a regulation
volleyball at a goalie who is protecting a lacrosse net with everything he's got . . . except his hands. There's an offense and a
defense, each patrolling its half of the field. You can dribble, kick,
or throw the ball. You can tackle, check, blindside, deliver forearm*

shivers, trip, spit on, and generally mutilate your opponent. The only difference between a combat exercise and a fieldball game is the absence of weapons. Gladiators in ancient Rome had easier days than a group of midshipmen battling it out on Hospital Point.

Only those midshipmen who feel they're indestructible play fieldball. What most ex-fieldballers remember about the game are the ever-present corpsmen, doctors, and ambulances. The hapless victims of sandwich plays, brutal blocks, and leg whips were always being carried off the field on stretchers and driven over to the nearby hospital for treatment.

Fortunately, midshipmen at the Naval Academy never have to worry about medical treatment. In the case of injury or illness, there's a gaggle of physicians, surgeons, and dentists on staff, along with plenty of corpsmen, nurses, and physician's assistants—not to mention a hospital, a pharmacy, full dental facilities, and state-of-the-art examining rooms. Everything from orthopedic surgery and antibiotics to yanking out wisdom teeth, all provided free of charge courtesy of good old Uncle Sam.

With that kind of medical coverage, you can play fieldball and hope to survive!

Along with all the other adventures you'll encounter while you're away at school, you'll have the task of ministering to your own health. Before you left home, being injured or sick was a snap. Mom or Dad was there to take care of you, drive you to the family doctor, and pick up your prescription at the neighborhood pharmacy. The greater part of your sick days was spent resting, perfecting your Nintendo skills, and channel-checking the TV. And the best part was that your parents paid for everything—prescriptions, doctor's bills, maybe even Super Mario Brothers 3.

Now when you wake up and feel miserable or sprain an ankle in a pick-up basketball game, you have to deal with it yourself. And getting sick or injured is neither fun nor cheap.

What health services are provided by your school? What is the cost of on- and off-campus health care? Should you enroll in the school's health care insurance program? Should you still be covered by your parents' health care plan? What are the key differences in various health insurance plans? Will you be covered by a health plan if you're working? Here's the run-down on health care and what to do when you're feeling run down.

Bumps, Bruises . . .

"College students are a remarkably healthy group," says David Christensen, Director of Student Health Services at Rutgers University in New Jersey.

In fact, most college on-campus medical facilities are set up to handle only the ordinary, everyday medical problems: flu, chest and head colds, and other viral infections, as well as athlete's foot, abrasions, sprained ankles and the like. They can also perform routine medical procedures like gynecological exams.

Under a simple student health plan, most colleges and universities will charge you a per-semester fee for providing this basic ambulatory care. Ambulatory care means that you "amble" into the campus clinic or health facility with a run-of-the-mill medical problem. Again, these are minor medical problems. More serious problems are referred to local hospitals or urgent care facilities. X-Rays, prescriptions and lab tests are usually extra, although they're priced very reasonably.

The cost of these programs is relatively low due to the demographics. The same use of statistics that worked against you for your car insurance comes to the rescue when the subject is health. Young adults between the ages of 18 and 25 rarely see a doctor except for routine examinations, a bad cold, flu, or an occasional bump, bruise, or break.

At Washington State University, for example, students are charged a mandatory student health fee of $50 per semester, $100 for the school year. On the east coast, at Rutgers, students are charged $48.50 per semester, but this fee also includes a small medical insurance policy which provides up to $2,500 per medical event.

You can expect to be charged something for the privilege of feeling rotten at the on-campus clinic. But what if you mess up your back in a major skiing accident? And who pays for it?

And Breaks . . .

University health centers typically are not equipped to handle major medical needs such as back surgery. Major medical problems are usually referred to local hospitals.

Back surgery can cost thousands of dollars: there are separate fees for the surgeon, anesthesiologist, hospital room, medicine, physical therapy, and so on. Your school's health insurance plan is not likely to cover these big-ticket items; your coverage may be limited to a small amount, perhaps $2,500, and only apply to certain services. The fact is, most on-campus medical professionals are going to assume that you're also covered by some kind of outside medical insurance.

In most cases, you'll be covered by your parents' health care insurance plan. Family health plans typically cover dependent children until the end of the year in which they turn 19. And, according to Susan Miller, a health care professional formerly with Blue Cross, about 90% of the plans will continue to provide for dependent children until age 23 or 25 as long as they receive at least 50% support from their parents. Check your parents' plan before you head off into the great beyond. Make sure you're covered.

What if you're making it on your own and aren't covered by your parents' policy?

You can buy your own. Fortunately, many schools offer a student health care insurance policy that covers serious medical problems. Remember, this is above and beyond the basic ambulatory care package for on-campus health care. And once again, these program are fairly reasonable in cost.

How much coverage and what benefits you get will vary from school to school and policy to policy. It's crucial not only to have insurance, but to understand your particular policy, what it covers and what it doesn't.

Let's look at one university's plan in more detail.

Here's the Plan

DePaul University is located in inner-city Chicago. Although some students live on campus, DePaul is a popular commuter college. DePaul does not offer on-campus health services, but is instead affiliated with nearby Grant Hospital, a major metropolitan health center. Sick students receive care at Grant Hospital and payment is expected by filing with your insurance company (or your parents' insurance company). For those not covered by a plan, DePaul University offers a Student Health Insurance Plan.

For a single student, the cost of Plan I, the Basic Accident and Sickness Program Benefits, is $243 for one full calendar year, September 1 to September 1. There is a deductible of $50. This means you pay the first $50 for medical care before the insurance company begins sharing costs. Under this plan, you are covered for any one injury or sickness up to $20,000, including up to $5,000 in hospital protection.

Once you reach the $50 deductible, you begin to receive benefits from the plan. However, the Student Health Insurance Plan does not defray all of your medical costs. Instead, you share these costs. The plan picks up 80% of the cost and you pay the remaining 20%.

Here's an example. A sophomore Blue Demon wakes up one morning and heads off to an aerobics class. On the way, she slips on a patch of ice and sprains her wrist. Seeing a silver lining in this dark cloud, she rationalizes her way out of her calculus class and marches over to Grant Hospital. There she is examined, X-rayed, taped, and sent on her way with a prescription for Tylenol with codeine. The visit to the emergency room costs $127.20. Assuming she has already paid her $50 deductible, she will pay $25.44 and the Student Health Insurance will pay $101.76. ($127.20 X .80 = $101.76)

Let's get "back" to that skiing injury. Back surgery is covered under the "Major Medical Expense Benefit" of the plan. The plan will pay 80% of all "reasonable and customary" expenses in excess of $100 up to a maximum of $15,000 for any one injury or sickness. An additional $5,000 in hospital protection is offered; this covers the hospital room, physician's treatment, ambulance service, nursing care, and other hospital expenses. If the bill for the back surgery is $8,350, including the hospital stay and ongoing physical therapy, you will be expected to pay 20% of the bill (and the first $100), or $1,770. ($8,350 X .20 + $100 = $1,770.)

The trouble with school policies is that they may be less inclusive than you want. You need to read each plan very carefully. With the DePaul plan, for example, benefits will not be paid for a host of medical problems. Dental treatment is excluded, unless this treatment results from an injury to your "natural teeth." The plan will not cover having a cavity filled, but if you catch a Louisville Slugger to the chops, you're safe—toothless perhaps, but safe. Eyeglasses, contact lenses, or eye examinations are not covered. Nor will the plan pay for preventive medicines, vaccines, cosmetic surgery, injuries sustained in an aviation accident except for passengers of commercial airlines, intentionally self-inflicted injuries, elective abortions or sterilizations, or pre-existing conditions.

Beware the pre-existing condition. If you have been previously diagnosed with diabetes, or hypertension, or skin cancer, or any other condition which requires ongoing treatment, this treatment will be excluded from your plan.

Another concern is what would happen if your medical bills exceeded the insurance. You can also purchase a "catastrophic health insurance policy" which would pay for catastrophic illness or surgeries. The deductible is usually $15,000 or $20,000 and the policy kicks in where your other policy leaves off. Again, good news for students: this insurance is relatively inexpensive.

Workin' 9 to 5

If you work full-time while attending college, or work part-time for a truly enlightened and generous employer, you may find yourself covered by the company's health insurance plan. These plans vary.

Three popular health plans available today are: HMO, PPO, and Fee-for-Service. Sometimes companies offer you only one type, and sometimes you have a choice.

HMO: Health Maintenance Organization

An HMO is the medical equivalent of circle-the-wagons. A hospital, a group of hospitals, (Kaiser Permanente, for example), and a staff of physicians join forces to provide health services. Instead of receiving payment for each service rendered, HMOs charge a pre-arranged amount of money per month through a health insurance company or their own membership with patients.

One of my friends at work sees a $32 deduction from his pay-check each month. However, he pays a nominal fee of $2 for each appointment with an HMO physician. That's $2, whether it's for a hernia, a chest X-ray, or a sore throat. "It's like going to the $2 window at the racetrack," he muses. "The big payoff is that I haven't been really sick."

Because the HMO's fees are fixed on a per-patient basis, the emphasis is on health maintenance—in other words, keeping you healthy so that more expensive procedures will not have to be performed down the road. For example, in the course of a physical your physician discovers that your cholesterol level is 285—dangerously high. By treating you now, helping you change your eating habits, restricting fat in your diet, counseling, and perhaps even medicating the problem, the HMO seeks to avoid the quadruple bypass you might need when you're 55.

The tradeoffs: You must use an HMO group physician, and there is usually a reduced number or X-rays and laboratory tests performed. However, even the tradeoff has a tradeoff. "Many people hold the opinion that unnecessary tests are performed in fee-for-service plans," says health care professional Miller. Excessive tests run up expensive bills, so the leap of faith here is that HMOs will perform only the laboratory tests necessary to treat a given condition.

PPO: Preferred Provider Organization

Like an HMO, a PPO is a group of doctors who have joined forces to provide a spectrum of medical services for a fixed fee. This relatively new development in the health insurance industry allows patients to choose a doctor, as long as that doctor is on its participant list. Doctors like the plan because they get continuous referrals. The insurance company likes it because it can contain costs by limiting what it will reimburse doctors. Patients like PPOs because direct costs to them are limited, although not eliminated. One drawback for patients is that if you use a doctor outside the network, your out-of-pocket cost will be higher.

Fee-for-Service

Fee-for-service plans will pay a large percentage of medical expenses regardless of the doctor chosen. However, fee-for-service plans normally require deductibles and co-payments for services like office visits, prescriptions drugs, medical equipment, and supplies. Co-payment means that you share the cost. For example, if you see a physical therapist at $60 per hour, you may pay 20%, or $12, each visit, while the insurance company pays the rest.

Employers usually offer these plans under the aegis of a major medical insurance company such as Blue Cross, Blue Shield, Aetna, Prudential, Metropolitan, and The Equitable. Although these companies also provide individual health care policies, they usually concentrate on group health plans.

Sickness d' Jour

Covered by mom and dad's policy (or your own) and paid-in-full for on-campus ambulatory care, you're ready to get sick and test the system. Here's a list of the common ailments you may encounter while matriculating, most of which will be treated at the student health center:

1. Respiratory infections: Number one at most on-campus health clinics, this category is a catch-all for everything from influenza to the common cold, from bronchitis to strep throat. "These are infections you can't do much to avoid," says Captain Gabe Lombard, USN, Brigade Medical Officer at the U.S. Naval Academy. Captain Lombard and his staff see a particularly large number of viral infections in the two weeks following the Brigade's return from vacation. "The midshipmen come back to school after having been exposed to every kind of bug and virus from the four corners of the USA," he explains.

2. Sexually transmitted diseases. Sexually transmitted diseases (genital herpes, venereal warts, syphilis, gonorrhea, and AIDS) are a medical problem on most U.S. college campuses. "The fact is the student body is immensely active," says Rutgers' David Christensen. And it's apparent that these students are not practicing safe sex. "At Rutgers we have about 85,000 patient visits a year," says Christensen. "About 4,000 of those visits are for sexually transmitted diseases." The Rutgers student body is composed of about 30,000 full-time students and 17,000 part-time students.

Virginia Moore, a nurse practitioner at Creighton University's Health Center, agrees that sexually transmitted diseases are a major problem on campuses. "We need to look at ways of getting through to the students and educating them to reevaluate their sexual practices. You can't be encouraged when you look at the nationwide statistics."

3. Gynecological visits: "About a third of our cases are gynecological in nature," reports Christensen "These clinic visits include routine examinations and PAP smears, as well as prescribing oral contraceptives."

The Naval Academy's Captain Lombard reports that in addition to regular gynecological examinations and treatments, menstrual problems brought on by excessive physical demands are quite common. "The level of physical activity for the average woman midshipman rivals that of an elite, world-class athlete," says Lombard.

4. Orthopedic problems. Orthopedic problems include assorted bumps, bruises, lacerations, sprains, and breaks. Sports injuries plague a significant percentage of a representative student population, both male and female. Athletes, especially scholarship athletes, are most concerned about sports-related (and perhaps career-ending) injuries. Many schools have ancillary programs for athletes. Training rooms, physical therapy rooms, team physicians, orthopedic surgeons, and the like, abound. However, sports injuries migrate to the intramural, or "pick-up" level. While many of these injuries result in simple "R-I-C-E" therapy (Rest, Ice, Compression, Elevation), some are serious enough to warrant X-ray examinations and physical therapy. Other more serious trauma, such as compound fractures, are also no strangers to campus health centers.

The medical problems of college students are no different from the problems of the public at large. Says Christensen, "We see the same problems that most general practices encounter."

Programs To Be Proud Of

Some of the on-campus health centers have expanded their services to be more responsive to changing student needs.

Creighton University's Moore is especially proud of the immunization program that has been instituted on the Omaha, Nebraska campus. "We immunize for two types of measles, rubella and rubeola, as well as mumps," says Moore. "Rubeola outbreaks have occurred on college campuses. For our program, immunization is a requirement. If it's not completed by the second semester, we withhold registration."

Moore also discusses a lifestyle assessment program recently implemented at Creighton. This program deals with important lifestyle choices and disorders that have lasting effects on the students' health. Some of these include the effects of smoking, the consequences of eating disorders like anorexia nervosa and bulemia, and the dangers of alcohol abuse. After self-evaluation, a student may elect to enter a voluntary treatment program provided by the student health center, the counseling center, the drug and alcohol counselor, or the Kiewet Fitness Center. Or the student may choose an off-campus treatment center.

Some of these specialized services are also offered on campus at Rutgers University, where a revolutionary 15-bed substance abuse program treats those with alcohol and drug abuse problems. "Alcohol is still the drug of choice," comments Christensen, "but most of our kids come to us as poly-drug users. They are abusing alcohol and cocaine, or alcohol and speed." The New Jersey State Health Department approved the Rutgers program. "We are considered a state resource," continues Christensen. "In addition to treating our own students, we had the larger population in mind."

A unique feature of Rutgers' program is the Sociology of Alcohol class that is taught while students are in-patients (patients remain "in" the facility during treatment) of the program. This accredited course serves two purposes: (1) it takes an academic look at the problems of substance abuse, and (2) it allows the student to continue being a student.

Often when a college student becomes an in-patient at a licensed substance abuse facility, he'll miss that semester. To avoid a glaring "hole" in the student's resume, Rutgers gives the student continuity. The Rutgers program even allows the student to re-enter the general student population and continue his regular coursework, albeit only one or two courses.

The out-patient treatment helps the student keep going after in-patient treatment is done. An "out-patient" continues treatment, but outside the facility. He is housed with other former abusers who work together to remain "clean."

Peer pressure may have helped cause the substance abuse problem, but it can also help in the effective treatment.

In Contusion . . .

With medical technology advancing to unparalleled levels, treatment costs have soared. Health insurance helps pay for this expensive care. It's not a question of whether you think you need this insurance coverage—you do. The question is which type of policy will suit you the best.

You obviously won't select your school based on student health facilities and the services offered. However, when you're choosing between private health insurance and school insurance, it's wise to compare. These group policies are often quite inexpensive relative to other health care insurance programs. And school coverage may be more comprehensive than you'd think.

PLANES, TRAINS, BUSES, AND AUTOMOBILES

▼ ▼ ▼

Cliff's most memorable road trip was during semester break. He and Dale were driving from Salt Lake City, Utah, to Washington, D.C. "Our car exploded in Medicine Bow, Wyoming," Cliff recalls. "Medicine Bow was a real one-horse town. Not only were we unable to find anyone to fix the car, there wasn't even a bus that stopped in town! We went back to the highway and practically threw ourselves in front of a passing bus, climbed on, and returned to Salt Lake. There we found a guy who was willing to drive back with us in his truck. He obligingly towed the car 200 miles before we found a mechanic who could fix it." By this time, Cliff was 5 days into an 11-day break...and broke. Exasperated, he

called home and had his father wire him enough money to take a
bus the rest of the way home. Dale and car made it to D.C. three
days later.

"Then on the return trip—same car, by the way," Cliff says,
"we stopped at a light in Kearney, Nebraska. A trooper came over
and told us that we had been speeding and that it was a $40 fine.
But between us we had only $15. When the trooper found out that
Dale's dad would wire the money for the fine, he led us back to the
station, where we spent the night locked in a cell waiting for the
bank to open the next morning."

"Most exciting trip I ever took," sighs Cliff.

Traveling to school, or home from school, can be an adventure.
In the interests of thrift and frugality, many a student gathers
experiences that become the stuff of humorous anecdotes. But the
stuff of anecdotes is rarely funny while it's happening.

How can you determine which means of travel will work best
for you? How do you comparison-shop for airfares? Are travel
agents really necessary? What are the advantages of riding the train,
taking the bus, ridesharing, and driving?

Travel can be filled with surprises, some unpleasant if you fail
to plan ahead and pay attention to detail. Keep in mind, a prepared
traveler is a happy traveler.

The Last Detail

Cost is often the single most important and obvious factor in determining how you'll get from school to home, and back again. But
you might want to ask yourself some other questions as well:

▼ *How far do you have to travel and how much time do you*
have to make the journey?

Consider a trip from San Francisco to Seattle. A drive along the
beautiful Pacific Coast would be fun, but do you have the time? Is
the journey too exhausting for you if it extends into days?

▼ *Is your destination easily accessible by your preferred method of transportation?*

In other words, can you get there from here? You may prefer the romance of traveling by train, but if the nearest depot is a two-hour drive from your destination, it may be easier for you to get there by bus or car.

▼ *Are you traveling alone or with friends?*

If you have traveling companions, their schedules could affect yours. You may be able to fuse your hands to the steering wheel and drive for hours on end, but others won't.

▼ *What method of travel is most convenient?*

Some airports are an hour or more away from your home or school. For example, a trip from New York City to Boston by air may be more trouble than it's worth. The airport may be accessible, but the mode of transportation is hardly convenient. Given the time it will take to drive to the airport, board the plane, fly, disembark, locate your luggage, and drive to your final destination, it would be easier to get to Boston by car.

▼ *What is the most comfortable mode of transportation for you?*

Does the thought of flying cause you to hyperventilate? Do you get carsick? Does your back ache for three days after a bus ride? Is it impossible for you to sleep on a train?

▼ *What's the most fun?*

The mode of transportation you choose doesn't have to be just the means to any end. It can be as much of an adventure as any of your vacations or breaks. A car trip along secondary roads will take more time than traveling the tollways and super highways, but enjoying the scenery, eating at roadside diners, and sightseeing in small towns may be a lot of fun.

Once you've answered all these questions and reached some decisions, there are some other factors to think about before you embark on your great journey. Suppose, for example, you're heading home for midterm break, flying from UCLA in Los Angeles to Denver, Colorado. You're wearing your neon-colored tank top and

Sideout shorts. This outfit might make the scene in LA, but you'll freeze to death upon arrival in Denver. Obviously, you forgot something, like what Denver Decembers are like.

To keep yourself from forgetting important details, consider where you're going, what you'll do when you get there, and what you have to take with you. Then make a list and check it twice. Clothes, toiletries, shoes, books, gifts, magazines, money, and tickets are only some of the things that may appear on the list. You should prepare for these travels as if you were preparing for finals. Your decisions should be made, plans verified, reservations checked, tickets in hand, bags packed...all the little questions answered. How are you getting to the airport or train station? Who's picking you up on the other end? What's the weather like?

NOBODY'S PERFECT

I remember a trip I took when I forgot to pack my underwear. This was not insurmountable as problems go, but it was an annoyance. And for a student on a budget, there were a lot of things other than underwear I would rather have purchased.

Then there was the time I arrived at Baltimore Friendship Airport in time to catch my flight. The only problem was that my flight was departing from Washington National Airport. Twenty years later, my father still regales his friends with that story.

The Friendly Skies

In the good old days, undergraduates depended on student discounts and standby travel. In today's deregulated world of air travel, you can't do the same. But there are some things you can do to save money on airfare.

As far as reservations go:

COMPARISON-SHOP If you choose to make the reservations yourself, take advantage of the toll-free telephone number most airlines offer. Savvy travelers shop the fares between airlines to find the best discounts. All it takes is a telephone call to the airlines and questions about the fares.

SEEK OUT THE BEST DEALS . . . EARLY The early bird get the best terms. Booking your flight as early as possible will often save you money. Don't wait until the last minute to make a reservation; if you do, you'll be charged top dollar. The difference in price between purchasing a ticket 14 days in advance and the day before a scheduled flight can be over 200%

CHECK RESTRICTIONS ON DISCOUNT FARES Most discount fares require advance purchase of between 7 and 30 days. This means that payment is required in advance. For the most part, these fares are nonrefundable. The airline reservationist will inform you that if you cancel the ticket, you may lose all your money.

NOTE: There are often other restrictions on discount tickets. You may be required to stay over a Saturday night or spend a minimum number of days before returning to the city where you began your travel. Other discount tickets require that you leave and/or return on certain days.

BE FLEXIBLE Flexibility in your travel plans can mean big savings. When you discuss your travel plans with the airline ticket reservationist, be organized and know what factor is the most important: price, time, or convenience. If you can delay your departure by one day, or travel very early in the morning or late at night, you may find a better fare.

CHECK THE NEWSPAPERS When making your reservations, check the travel section of the newspaper or ask the airline if it is currently running any special fares to specific cities. Often when an airline adds a new destination, or is attempting to encourage travel to one particular destination, special fares are offered. You might get lucky: that city just might be home, or near school.

Also sign up for airline frequent flyer programs, such as American Airline's AAdvantage Program, Delta Air Line's Frequent Flyer, and US Air's Frequent Traveler. If you're an "infrequent" frequent flyer, it might take you years to rack up the miles necessary for a free round-trip ticket. However, these mileage points can also be accumulated by staying at affiliated hotels, renting cars, and even using certain credit cards. And most airlines will start you off with bonus miles when you enroll in their program.

Get to the airport early. Overbooking is a common nemesis for travelers. If you don't get to the airport the hour or so before takeoff suggested by ticket agents, you might lose your seat. Yes, airlines will sell more tickets than there are seats for on the aircraft. Why? Because some passengers won't show—they've missed connections, changed travel plans, etc. Actually, overbooking can be a blessing in disguise—if you have flexibility in your travel plans. Airlines will often offer travel vouchers good for $200 to $500, or a free round-trip ticket valid for the next year, to volunteers who leave the overbooked aircraft and agree to take a later flight. Sometimes, meal vouchers and a night at a hotel are given if you're forced to take a flight that doesn't leave until the next day. If you absolutely have to make that flight, then get there early and check in.

Other Tips for Infrequent Flyers

LUGGAGE TAGS Make sure that your checked luggage has luggage tags, filled out with your name and address. Most airlines provide tags free of charge. It's better to have the tags filled out and affixed to your luggage before you get to the airport. Make sure your name and address are inside the bags as well. If your luggage is lost and the luggage tag has been torn away, an inside tag will help the airline identify your bag as yours. Some travelers further ID their luggage with patterns of masking tape, pom-poms, colored yarn, etc.

BAGGAGE CLAIM TICKETS When you check your luggage, most airline ticket agents will staple your baggage claim tickets to your ticket folder. Don't lose this folder! Even if you're on the last leg of your trip, hang on to these claim tickets. Most airports have stringent security at the baggage claim areas, matching your claim tickets to the actual tags on the luggage. Save time and embarrassment by having your claim tickets on hand.

MISSED CONNECTIONS   If you miss your connecting flight, find a ticket agent as soon as you get off the plane. Usually the airline is already aware of your problem and will have an agent stationed at the gate when you arrive. These agents will help you find another flight to complete your travel plans.

There is traveling, and there is traveling well. You shouldn't ignore creature comforts when you travel. The age-old question of "Window or aisle?" is usually answered by considering where you're more comfortable. Do you want to crawl over people or be crawled over? Do you want a view out of that window?

There are also some choices to be made concerning airline food. Airlines have become very sensitive to the special dietary needs of their passengers. Kosher, low-sodium, vegetarian, lactate-free vegetarian, seafood, and other special diet meals are available. Simply call the airline at least 24 hours in advance and request the meal. This service doesn't cost you extra!

Riding the Rails

Traveling by train may prove to be more economical than flying. There is a tradeoff, however. While an airplane can get you across the United States in just under five hours, the train takes three days.

If you have the time, or the inclination, train travel may be more your style. You can walk around, even get off at stops along the way; you'll see the country at ground level; and trains travel to remote destinations.

AMTRAK, the nation's train service, offers a variety of programs and fares. When you call, ask for special excursion fares. The round-trip excursion fare between Chicago and Los Angeles is about half that of the best airfare. AMTRAK also offers its "All

Aboard America" package. Loosely based on the Eurail Pass, the AMTRAK program allows the traveler three stops and the return trip over a 45-day period. The fare is priced by region (AMTRAK has divided the country into three regions: East, Middle, and West), and the more regions you travel to under this program the more it costs.

Bus Stop

One of the most economical methods of transportation is by bus. Fares are very reasonable. Moreover, buses travel where airplanes and trains don't. Greyhound Bus Lines, a national bus company, also offers discount fares during Spring Break. (Now there's a traveler's nightmare—a busload of students on their way to Fort Lauderdale!)

Greyhound offers its AmeriPass program, which allows you travel anywhere in the Greyhound system in the United States or Canada for a 7-, 15-, or 30-day period. You can even buy additional days on this fare. For example, the 15-day pass costs $259, and you can purchase up to 14 additional days at $10 each. You don't have to buy the additional days when you first purchase your AmeriPass. Instead, you have the flexibility to custom-tailor your pass. In addition to Greyhound, there are other, regional, bus lines which may suit your needs.

A word of caution. Bus stations are rarely located in the most upscale parts of town, and they tend to draw a rather seedy crowd. So, be careful and alert.

On the Road Again

The classic American home-from-school (or back-to-school) experience is the road trip. A bunch of students pile into a car or van with everything they own and take off. Road trips can be a lot of fun, or they can be nightmares. Often the only difference is a bit of prior planning.

A visit to an Automobile Association of America (AAA) office might be in order. Membership in AAA can be very practical. Roadside assistance, towing, travel services, discounts, and trip planning are only a few of the benefits of being a AAA member.

You obviously know where you're going before you begin the road trip. So, go into the local AAA office and ask them to plan out your trip. They will give you the route to take, estimate the time it will take to complete the legs of the trip, and, if it's a long trip, even make recommendations on where to spend the night. Should anything happen to your car during the trip, roadside assistance is available. In addition, many motels and hotels offer discounts to AAA members.

A bit of preventive maintenance is also in order. Check the car's radiator, oil, brake fluid, windshield wiper solvent, and transmission fluid. Make sure the tires are properly inflated, with special attention paid to the spare. If scheduled service for the car is needed, get it done before any long trip.

It's also a good idea to have money—both cash and traveler's checks—to pay for minor things like food and gas. Why not all traveler's checks? You can't use traveler's checks at a toll booth, candy machine, or parking meter.

Most schools have ridesharing boards. Students looking for someone to share the driving duties, or just trying to find a way home, advertise on these boards. To make your ridesharing road trip relatively hassle-free, ask the following questions:

Will I have to drive?
What expenses will I expected to share?
Where will you drop me?
Will I be required to navigate?
Are you planning to drive straight through or do we stop?
What about meals?
Is it a smoking or non-smoking car?
How many people will be traveling?
How do you feel about drinking and driving?

Getting this stuff out into the open should prevent any false expectations or misconceptions. In terms of road trip etiquette, you should expect to pay your own way, and this means paying for your share of gas. You may be expected to share the driving. And you'll probably be expected to provide some entertainment—it pays to be great conversationalist or have a huge collection of really great cassette tapes.

Here are some other road trip tips:

▼ Pack a snack. It will surprise you how much money you can save by loading up the cooler with sandwiches and fruit, rather than sampling the truck stop menus.

▼ While you're eating, park the car where you can see it, whether you're having a roadside picnic or a candlelit dinner at the diner.

▼ Bring some water. You and your car may get very thirsty on a very remote, very hot, very dry section of road.

DRIVE AWAY

You can actually drive someone else's car home. Under "Automobile Transporters and Drive Away Companies" in the local Yellow Pages, the enterprising student will find a list of companies that specialize in this form of auto transport. Private individuals or companies contract with these services to have their cars driven to a final destination. These companies then screen applicants and provide a driver. (NOTE: You have to be at least 21 years old to even think about applying.)

Let's say you're attending UC Santa Barbara and you want to get back home to Chicago, Illinois. You locate a drive-away company in Los Angeles that has a delivery to make in Chicago. They will send you an in-depth application, which requires a photograph and fingerprints. References, driving experience, and driving records must be provided. If you are hired and given a car to drive, you will also be required to leave a cash deposit. The deposit is returned to you when you deliver the car. The car is given to you with a full tank of gas, but from then on you're on your own.

▼

▼ Seasoned road warriors carry their own toilet paper and tissues—just in case.

▼ Empty the car if you're spending the night at a motel or a friend's house. Don't leave suitcase, boxes, or other belongings in the car, even in the trunk. Never leave gift-wrapped boxes, camera cases, videocams, or money in plain view.

▼ Lock your car doors, even if you're only running inside to pay the cashier for gas.

The Secret (Travel) Agent

"Most students think it costs them more money to work with a travel agent," says Regina Schneider, Marketing Manager at Rosenbluth Travel Agency, Inc., one of the nation's largest travel management firms. "That's simply not true. The travel agent receives her commission from the airline, or hotel, or tour promoter, not from the customer."

In fact, travel agents (or, in today's parlance, "travel consultants") can save you money.

Travel agents are aware of what's going on in the travel market. They know where to find travel bargains. Travel agents can deal with all the airlines and find you the best fare. They can also help you with any special needs. Agents are vast repositories of travel advice and tips.

By using a travel agent, you receive professional service and advice and still pay the same price for your airfare. "Travel agents also give out advice on destinations, provide literature, and put together package deals," continues Schneider. "Also, as a customer, you can take advantage of the purchasing power and clout that your travel agent has in the market."

Travel agents provide other services as well. For example, Rosenbluth has a 24-hour emergency service toll-free telephone number. "Should you lose your luggage, miss a connection, or get stranded," says Schneider, "we can help." Schneider suggests putting that toll-free number on your luggage tag. If your lost luggage is recovered, the baggage department of the airline will call the travel agency. Because they know your itinerary, the travel agency then helps re-route the luggage to you.

How can you be sure that an agency is delivering the lowest fare available? Ask the agent if they offer a guarantee. Some travel agents will guarantee the lowest fare. Some have access to all the airline reservation computer systems, while others build their own system which integrates the entire network. Even small agencies have the capability to search for the lowest fares. If you find an agency that relies on one airline's computer reservation system, you might find that you'll be shown a preponderance of that airline's flights in your travel plans. Ask, investigate, then decide.

Travel agents also have first-hand knowledge about many destinations. They'll recommend the best airport when a traveler heads to New York City. LaGuardia, Kennedy, or Newark? Let the agent help you. If you need document assistance (passports, visas, immunization/inoculations), ask your agent.

By keeping track of what's happening in the industry, a travel agent can save you more than money. "In early 1990 there was a hotel workers' strike in Hawaii which affected many travelers," explains Schneider. "We were able to advise our customers about the strike and recommend hotels which weren't affected."

It also helps if you provide information that will make it easier for the travel agent to assist you. For example, when you call to make airline reservations, have the departure and return dates available. What seating do you prefer? Are special meals needed? Do you have to travel at a certain time of the day? What credit card will you be using? Are you a member of the frequent flyer program for that airline? Hotels? Rental cars? The agent will appreciate the preparation time that you take before you call.

"The student should know what's really important for his particular situation," counsels Schneider. "Ask yourself what is most important: cost, convenience, or time. These factors often have a major impact on the flight you'll take."

Most agents will build a computer file for each customer. Airline preference, method of payment, and other information are all kept in this file. Like any other service professional, a travel agent who keeps informed—and has a long, continuing relationship with a client—will provide the best service.

INVESTING FOR
THE FUTURE

▼ ▼ ▼

When she received a $1,500 inheritance from her grandmother,
Dori was ready to make her first investment in the stock market.
She turned to Craig, a family friend, for assistance. A recent college graduate, Craig was a brand-new broker, one of the many
new brokers hired by Wall Street at a time when it looked like the
market would go up forever. He convinced Dori that he could help
her pick stocks that would make money for her. After all, Craig had
been making money for his clients and he felt an obligation to do
the same for a friend of the family.

Dori's instructions to the newest maven of Wall Street were
simple. "Invest the money wherever you think best." And Craig did

just that. His first trade on Dori's behalf—100 shares of a consumer products stock purchased at $15 a share, did make money. The stock rose to over $19 and Dori's initial investment was now worth $1,900. So, on Craig's advice, she sold and reinvested the money in a speculative oil and gas company. She was able to buy over 500 shares of this relatively inexpensive stock. In short order, Dori's second investment lost a few points, but Craig wasn't worried, so neither was Dori. Dori had more pressing things to worry about; and besides, Craig was the expert . . . he knew what he was doing. They discussed the stock's drop in price, and Craig agreed to watch it for awhile. If the stock's price improved or worsened, he would get in touch and they would talk again.

In the meantime, a number of Craig's other sensational picks took a turn for the worse. Like many new brokers, Craig had confused genius with a bull market. As the stocks he selected started losing value, he began to regret not only his recommendations but his choice of career as well.

When Dori didn't hear from Craig, she finally called to see how her speculative oil and gas stock was faring. That's when she learned that Craig had quit to go to law school and that her $1,500 investment, after growing to nearly $1,900, was now worth about $500.

Dori's experience is not that unusual. Like Dori, many new investors play a high-stakes game early in their investing careers. They buy stocks recommended by barbers, cab drivers, and friends with "sure-fire tips." Even the recommendations of financial professionals don't always work out. Often investors who get burned turn sour on the stock market and never invest in stocks again. What was unusual about Dori's experience was that she later decided to enter the field of finance.

"I look back and I flinch," she says. "I can't believe I told him to do 'whatever' he thought was best. Worse, I put all my eggs in one basket, and then failed to watch that basket."

There are many paths to take on the road to financial independence—and the path of investments is paved with good intentions, strewn with obstacles, and marked by expensive naivete. And there are lots of people willing to lead you down that path. Literally hundreds of books offer surefire advice about investing in everything from real estate to stocks to commodities. Everyone has a method to beat the system, outperform the market, win without risk, win by taking extraordinary risk, win without putting any money down, and various and sundry other strategies . . . . But before you start, you might want to keep in mind the advice of an old broker who has an interesting hand-lettered sign hanging prominently in his office: "Investing is a process, not an event."

"This simple reminder keeps me humble," he says. "There's really no such thing as getting rich quick. A disciplined, intelligent approach to investing is the only way to go."

Should you be thinking about investing now? What are some appropriate investments for a college student? What shouldn't you invest in during these halcyon days? What exactly are stocks and bonds? What's a Treasury bill? What are junk bonds and why are they called that? What are mutual funds and money market funds?

The toughest task for a young investor trying to follow any financial planning advice is controlling the "I want it now!" urge. Building your investments can take years, but when you're in college, it's hard to see beyond your next paper, final, or vacation break. The thing is, it doesn't get any easier after college: the price tags just get higher—for the car, the Club Med vacation, the bedroom set, the power suit.

Which brings us to perhaps *the* question: Why should you invest your money at all?

The fact is, you invest and save to get something you want. Investing and saving work best when you have a particular financial objective or a clear-cut goal in mind. A new car, a downpayment on your first house, an education fund for your children, a vacation, and retirement are some of the common goals. You can achieve these and other goals through a variety of investment choices.

Despite the fact that you want it all now, it is by postponing purchases and saving money that most people build their wealth.

Ancient Egypt's Contribution to the World of Investing

Thousands of years after they were built as tombs for Egyptian pharaohs, the pyramids are still standing. How these pyramids were built remains a mystery, but everyone knows why they're still around. They were built on the principles of a strong foundation and balance.

In contrast, there is little mystery to the *investment pyramid*. Like its historical inspiration, the investment pyramid is also built to last on a strong foundation and balance. Stockbrokers, financial consultants, money managers, bankers, insurance representatives, and mutual fund salesmen will all trot out the investment pyramid during their presentations. They endeavor to convince new investors that these principles—a strong foundation and balance—create individual wealth. This means that, over time, using a foundation of conservative investments and a balance of progressively riskier investments, you can build your own pile of money.

Investing is simply a progression of trade-offs between risk and reward. The less you risk (or the less risky the investment), the lower the reward. Trite but true. "Nothing ventured, nothing gained" applies to investments as well.

So, in building the investment pyramid, you begin at the foundation, with safe, secure, and oftentimes insured investments. Then you build higher. The higher you build, the more risk you are willing to accept.

The Financial Foundation: Savings

What kind of investments make up the base, or foundation, of the investment pyramid? These investments must be relatively safe and liquid. Safety means preserving your capital—in other words, you don't want to lose your money. Liquidity means that you can get your hands on your money at any time. Real estate investments

might be safe (sometimes they're not), but they are definitely illiq-
uid—you can't get your hands on your money on short notice.

Some of the investments that fall into this safe and liquid category are :

Cash
Passbook Savings
Certificates of Deposit
U.S. Treasury Bills, Notes, and Bonds
Money Market Mutual Funds

Cash

Cash is the ultimate in safety and liquidity. However, if your
money's in your wallet or mattress, it's not earning interest—it isn't
growing. In times of inflation, when the cost of goods is rising, cash
actually loses value. Think about the mountain bike you bought
today for $179.99. Last year that same bike sold for $159.99. The
cash you used today is actually worth less (because it buys less)
than the cash you had last year.

Passbook Savings

If your cash is not at home but in a bank, it may be in passbook savings. Passbook savings are traditional savings accounts. Generally
they pay a rather modest rate of interest, 5.25% for example. There
are advantages to passbook savings. You can open a savings account
with a relatively small amount of money, and make frequent, small
deposits to it. You have access to that money at any time. Some
banks allow you to withdraw your savings through the Automatic
Teller Machine (ATM). Finally, your savings (up to $100,000) are
insured by the Federal Deposit Insurance Corporation (FDIC).

Certificates of Deposit, CDs

If your savings have grown into the thousands of dollars, you may
invest in certificates of deposit, or CDs, which "lock" up your

money for a set period of time. You can also purchase CDs from thrifts, savings & loans, and credit unions. Some brokerage houses—Merrill Lynch, Shearson Lehman Brothers, Paine Webber, etc.—also offer investors CDs. Certificates of deposit generally pay a fixed rate of interest for a fixed term. This rate is normally higher than you'd get on passbook savings. For example, you might deposit $5,000 and buy a six-month CD at 8.25%. At the end of the term, you'll receive $412.50 in interest ($5,000 X .0825/2 = $412.50). How do CDs differ from passbook savings? First, CDs are denominated in $1,000 increments. Second, the CD interest is paid on a term—three months, six months, one year, etc. Third, you can't get your hands on the money. If you need the money before the term of the CD expires, you have to pay a penalty—usually about one month's interest if the term of the CD is one year or less, and up to three months' interest if the term is longer than a year.

U.S. Treasury Bills, Notes, and Bonds

Considered the ultimate in safety are obligations backed by "the full faith and credit of the U.S. Government." Why? Because, when it issues *U.S. Treasury bills, notes,* and *bonds,* the government is borrowing money. Those who buy these government obligations actually lend the government money for a fixed rate of interest. In effect, unless this country collapses, Uncle Sam will honor all monies owed. The government issues securities for a variety of reasons: to make up the shortfall between revenues and expenditures (in other words, to finance the multi-trillion dollar debt caused by deficit spending), to finance student loans, to bail out the savings & loans, to provide low-cost mortgages for Armed Forces veterans, and so forth. The only difference between bills, notes, and bonds is the length of time until maturity. Bills mature in one year or less, notes under four years, and bonds as long as 30 years. Treasury bills require an initial investment of $10,000 and you can add to that in increments of $5,000, while Treasury notes and bonds require a $1,000 initial investment.

Money-Market Mutual Funds

From the ultimate in safety to the ultimate in liquidity, you might want to look into money-market mutual funds. The term "money market" describes a market for short-term, highly liquid investments ranging from U.S. Treasury bills and CDs, to commercial paper (IOU's issued by corporations), banker's acceptances (trade IOUs issued by banks in favor of an import/export customer), and other short-term investments. Short-term means that all these investments mature within 270 days. Many of these short-term securities require $100,000 to make a direct investment.

Don't have $100,000? That's OK, because you can still invest through money-market mutual funds, which pool the resources of many investors. You can open a money-market mutual fund account with as little as $1,000. These funds give you a return comparable to those of CDs, Treasury bills, and the like—and they also offer liquidity.

You can open a money-market fund at a variety of institutions: banks, savings & loans, thrifts, credit unions, mutual fund companies, and brokerage houses. Access to your money is generally though checks or "credit cards" issued against the account. These credit cards are actually debit cards—as the charge hits your account, it is automatically debited, or deducted, from your balance. Checks sometimes have a minimum ($500 is not unusual). The big advantage is that your money is available right now, and in the meantime it's earning a competitive return.

Because the money market itself is an ever-changing, true market, your return will fluctuate daily. As the general trend in interest rates goes, so goes the return of your money-market fund. Should interest rates trend up, the rate of return on your money fund should also rise. If rates come down, so does your return.

While these investments may not seem exciting, they provide an excellent foundation for long-term financial planning. Once you have a strong base built, you can advance your investing strategy to the next level, where growth is emphasized.

The Second Tier: Growth and Income

As you work your way up the investment pyramid, you begin to accept more risk, in hope of a better reward. Investments in the second tier of the investment pyramid include:

Investment-grade and good quality common stocks
Utility common stock
Investment-grade corporate bonds
Investment-grade municipal bonds

When you own stock in a company, you own "equity"—a part of that company. Owners of bonds, however, hold "debt"—a promise by the company to repay money borrowed from the bondholder.

Stock = owner = equity   Bonds = lender = debt

Let's take an example. You and two friends start a toy company. Hope is a great designer, Joy knows about manufacturing, and you're a super saleswoman. You each commit $2,000 toward startup costs, and you all sign an agreement, giving each of you thirty-three and one-third percent stock ownership in the fledgling company. Your mother, Charity, agrees to lend you $4,000. She's not interested in becoming an owner, but prefers to be a "banker," lending you the money at a 10% rate. She expects the loan to be fully paid back in three years. With $10,000, your company is born.

A year later, your trio is flush with success. After all expenses, the company has a profit of $42,000! The three of you decide to pay back your mom's loan in full with interest, draw a salary of $8,000 each, and plow the remaining money back into the company.

If your toy company continues to grow, you may need even more money to continue your expansion. You and your friends might decide to sell some of your stock to the public. When you do this, it's called "going public." Many successful companies now trading on stock exchanges and the over-the-counter market began just like this. Apple Computer was started by two self-proclaimed "computer nerds" who designed a portable home computer in a garage. Ray Kroc, the founder of McDonald's, began his multi-billion franchised food operation by buying a single hamburger stand!

Stocks

You might not be able to start a company, but you can do the next best thing. When you buy stock in a company, it's more than a chance to make or lose money. You become an owner. You may attend shareholder meetings and voice your opinion on how the company is being managed. (If you own enough stock, you can bet the board of directors will listen to you.) Best of all, stocks let you share in a company's profits. This can happen when the share price of a stock rises in the market, or when the company pays you a portion of its earnings in the form of a dividend.

Stocks can be either high-risk or low-risk. This usually depends on how long the company has been in business, how steadily its earning (profits) stream has grown, and how it fares against the competition. It can even depend on whether its product or service is seasonal or cyclical.

Investment-grade and good quality common stocks represent ownership in the top tier of corporations, also known as "blue chips." Some examples are General Motors, IBM, McDonald's, Disney, American Telephone & Telegraph (AT&T), and General Electric. These companies have long histories of growth. They manufacture or produce "trademark" type products—Cadillacs, PS2 computers, Big Macs, theme parks and movies, telephones and long-distance service, etc. Many investment-grade or good quality stocks pay quarterly dividends. These dividends represent a portion of the company's earnings, and are passed along to the owners, or holders, of stock.

Utility common stock has also been long considered a safe haven for investing. The local gas and electric company, the regional "Baby Bell" telephone company (Ameritech, BellSouth, and Pacific Telesis among others) are utility companies. Many stockbrokers refer to utility stocks as "widow and orphan" stocks, thus suggesting that they are safe and not prone to volatile price swings. Utility stocks usually pay an above-average dividend compared to other stocks.

Bonds

Also included in this level of the pyramid are certain corporate bonds. In the toy company example, mom was investing in a somewhat speculative venture—a start-up company—but choosing to do so by "acting as a banker." When you buy a corporate bond, you—like mom—are lending money to that corporation. You have reasonable expectations of being paid your coupon interest and repaid the principal at maturity.

High grade corporate bonds are the debt equivalents of investment-grade or good quality stocks. The corporation owes the bondholder money and pays a stated rate of interest, called the "coupon rate," twice a year. For example, if you buy $10,000 in bonds paying a 9% coupon, you receive $450 every six months ($10,000 X .09/2 = $450). The interest rate on these bonds is higher than that of government bonds with the same maturity. Why? Because corporate bonds are higher up the pyramid; there is more inherent risk, hence more reward. Instead of the U.S. Treasury, you now have the full faith and credit of General Motors, for example, backing the bond.

High grade municipal bonds are issued by states, cities, or municipal agencies to fund a variety of projects, such as prisons, rapid transit, airports, police stations, and bridges. Municipal bonds, or "munis," are attractive because the holder is exempt from paying federal, state, and local taxes on the interest received. Most of you won't be interested in "munis" yet. These bonds are purchased by individuals in high tax brackets.

The Third Tier:
Speculation and Peculation

Only when you have a strong foundation built should you begin thinking about investing for long-term growth and income. Once you have a healthy second level built, you are ready for the more speculative investments—the ones that involve real risk.

The third tier may include such investments as speculative common stock and lower quality bonds.

Speculative common stock provides ownership of smaller, "secondary" stocks in companies without the long track record or established products of "blue chip" companies. For those with the judgment to invest wisely, the patience to stick it out, and admittedly a bit of luck, investing in speculative stocks can be quite rewarding. New concepts or technologies fuel this market. Apple Computer, Microsoft, and Genentech are examples of companies once considered to be highly speculative for investors. These companies are considered to be "blue chip" investments in their respective industries; yet all came from very humble beginnings. Remember, for each success story there are hundreds, perhaps thousands, of "hard luck" stories about companies that have been "the next (fill in the blank)." You have to keep in mind that speculation is just that—you expect far greater returns because you have taken far greater risk.

Lower quality bonds, aka "junk bonds," are debts of financially weak corporations or municipalities. Many corporate issues of these lower (or lowest) grade bonds were issued during the mergers and acquisition binge of the 1980s. Companies would gobble up other companies, taking on loads of debt to finance the deal. It wasn't unusual to see coupons of 15%+, which was nearly twice the yield paid on Treasury bonds. Any investment nearly twice the standard return should be considered very high risk.

The Tip: Rolling the Dice

At the peak of the pyramid, up at the top where the air is rare, are high-risk investments. Take real estate, for example. Raw, undeveloped land is the north forty without a crop. No roads, sewer lines, utility service. Just land. Unless it's a choice bit of land (seven acres in Beverly Hills comes to mind), this is the kind of investment you can expect to hold onto for quite a long while before you make your fortune. This is also the kind of investment you should avoid. In fact, avoid the entire tip of the pyramid. Long options and commodities, for instance, are highly leveraged, very high-risk investments. Leverage means that you borrow money to make an investment. If the investment goes against you, you might lose more than you originally committed. Yes, savvy traders have made and will continue to make fortunes on these high-risk ventures. However, statistics show that over 90% of those who "play" this part of the market lose money—generally all the money they commit. Why buck the

RULES AND TOOLS

"Young people usually haven't got a lot of money to invest," observes Jay Rabinowitz of Merrill Lynch. "Given that, I'd recommend a mutual fund as the optimum investment vehicle. The mutual fund addresses the cardinal rule of investing—diversification. Spread the risk."

Rabinowitz has been with Merrill Lynch for over ten years. He has been involved in financial planning, estates planning, retirement planning, and corporate benefits. "Students should adopt the concept of dollar-cost averaging," he continues. "Dollar-cost averaging means putting away a fixed amount of money away each month. This amount may be modest, let's say $25, but the important thing is that it creates a discipline. The beauty of dollar-cost averaging is that you buy the selected investment at a range of prices. Let's say you're buying $25 worth of ABC Mutual Fund each month. The first month the shares are priced at $12.50 each and you buy two shares. The next month the price is $12.25, so you'll buy 2.04 shares. The third month the price is $12.75 and you buy 1.96 shares.

"This disciplined, steady investment program also helps avoid the two biggest obstacles to investors—fear and greed."

In fact, Merrill Lynch offers a unique investment program—The Blueprint Account—which is ideal for dollar cost averaging. This account allows you to make rather modest investments in stocks, money market funds, and mutual funds. For as little as $25, you can buy stock in IBM. Granted, it may only represent a fractional share of IBM, but through your dogged investment program and dollar cost

odds? Huge risk, huge potential reward . . . more often than not a
nuclear winter in your portfolio. What do you know about pork bel-
lies, frozen orange juice, Swiss francs, and board lumber, anyway?

The Glossary Continues

Here are a few more terms to help you learn the investment game.

Mutual funds combine the funds of many investors and use
this pool of money to invest along a specific policy as outlined in a

averaging, you can continue to accumulate IBM, or many other
investment choices.

Rabinowitz points out that, over time, the single best-perform-
ing investment has been the stock market. Over the past 50 years,
stocks have returned a compounded rate of return of 9%, better than
bonds, real estate, gold, or collectibles.

"The mistake most stock market novices make is that they try to
make money too quickly," Rabinowitz explains. "They want to make
a killing so they're willing to invest all their money in a penny stock
which has been touted as the next Apple Computer or the next IBM .
Usually they end up losing all their money and feel that the market is
too risky, or rigged, or some other such excuse which keeps them
away for the rest of their lives."

Rabinowitz is a believer in the investment pyramid. "It's never
too early to have a sound financial plan," he observes. "The investment pyramid helps you put that plan into a personal perspective."

"And remember," he cautions, "if it sounds too good to be true,
it probably is. Stay away from risky, leveraged investments, or 'sure
things.' "

Rabinowitz suggests that you try to identify themes in the mar-
ketplace and then determine how you can best capitalize on those
themes. For example, if you feel that concern for the environment will
be a major theme for the 1990s, then look at companies in the pollu-
tion control or waste management industries. You may even be able to
find a sector mutual fund that invests in just those types of companies.

prospectus. The prospectus explains the investment philosophy—"this fund seeks to achieve maximum return by investing in undervalued situations"—as well as noting any administrative, sales, and general charges. There are more mutual funds than there are stocks on the New York Stock Exchange. Some invest in certain industry sectors—high technology, medical, construction, etc.—while others invest in growth stocks, speculative stocks, Japanese stocks, European stocks, government bonds, corporate bonds, money markets, and on and on and on and on.

The advantages of mutual funds are: (1) professional management of the portfolio; (2) diversification (your relatively small investment is spread out over many different stocks or bonds); and (3) cost-effectiveness (it would be very difficult to duplicate the diversified portfolio on a micro-scale).

Precious metals, such as gold, silver, and platinum, are the investment of choice for some investors. Some investment managers recommend that most investors keep a small percentage of their assets in precious metals. The Europeans traditionally invest about 10% of their entire portfolio in precious metals. Precious metals provide an inflation hedge and ready currency in case of economic or political disaster. In the late 1970s and early 1980s, when double-digit inflation racked this country, gold reached $850 an ounce while silver hit over $50 an ounce.

You can invest in actual bullion through bars, or buy coins. Avoid investing in anything relating to precious metals where the come-on is "you can control $5,000 worth of platinum with an investment of $1,000!" This means leverage, and usually extraordinarily high commission charges.

Collectibles range from Old Masters' paintings to rare coins to baseball cards to stamps to antiques. Keep anything long enough and it becomes a collectible. The original Barbie doll, in her box, is worth a small fortune. Collectors rarely collect as an investment; they usually love the items they're collecting. The market conspires to turn their collectible into an "investable."

Keeping Up With the Dow Joneses

To select, and then monitor, your investments, you need information. Fortunately or unfortunately, there seems to be an information glut when it comes to investing. There is no substitute for knowledge, so you need to begin your quest by becoming familiar with the world of finance. Subscriptions to the *Wall Street Journal* or *Investor's Daily* will give you business news on a day-to-day basis. Magazines such as *Forbes, Business Week,* or *Money* also help. More serious investors will subscribe to an investment newsletter, or watch FNN (Financial News Network) or Wall $treet Week. You can also receive research from a brokerage house, or call a company directly to ask for an annual report.

For the diligent student of the market, there's always plenty to study. Remember the old adage, "Investigate before you invest."

APPENDIX:
FOUND MONEY

▼ ▼ ▼

Matthew Jared Klam had been tinkering with electrical appliances and electronic gadgets since he was a toddler. "While other kids crawled into bed with blankets," says his mother, Mary, "my two-year old went to sleep with wires."

Matt's second-grade teacher recognized the boy's fascination with electronics and introduced him to a repairman who worked at a nearby St. Vincent de Paul Center. They shared more than a love of tinkering and repairing appliances—neither Matt nor the repairman could hear.

Ten years later, Jean Eichman, Matt's science teacher at the Wis-consin School for the Deaf, encouraged him to enter a scholarship

*competition. The Duracell National Science Teachers Association
Scholarship awards money to students based on inventive uses for
batteries. Matt designed a walkie-talkie device for the hearing-
impaired, which he could use with his friends. He was one of five
second-place winners, each of whom received $3,000.*

*Matt is now attending Rochester Institute of Technology in
New York state, in the National Technical Institute for the Deaf.
Encouraged by his success in the hearing world, he plans to attend
RIT's engineering school with the help of a notetaker and a signer.*

Matt is no different from lots of other students who are trying
to find the financial resources to pay for college. For many
students financing a college education is a major challenge, maybe
the major challenge, of their lives. The annual costs at many top
private universities exceed $22,000, which means that your under-
graduate degree may come with an $88,000+ price tag. The cost of
attending a public university tends to be more reasonable, $6,000
to $8,000 a year, but that's still serious money. And if you think
that's a lot of money, wait until your little sister strolls through the
ivy-covered walls. Today's eight-year-old can expect to pay over
$110,000 for a private college!

What types of financing are available? How does financial aid
work? Where can you find out about scholarships offered by the
private sector? When should you start the great chase for money?

You shouldn't face this financing struggle alone. You're going
to need a team on this one. Many of the people you already
know—guidance counselors, teachers, coaches—can help you
make college happen. And you need to be the most valuable player on that team. The hunt for scholarship money, grants, and student loans will demand energy, dedication, and organization.

The Guide in the Financial Wilderness

Your first stop on the way to college should be the office of your
school's guidance counselor. Guidance counselors are perhaps your

most valuable asset in helping you select your college and finance your education. You may need to begin collecting letters of reference from teachers, family friends, alumni, and employers. There are financial profiles of your family to be completed, eligibility for work study to be determined, and scholarships to compete for. Your guidance counselor will be able to assist you. Mina Smith, a guidance counselor at South Mountain High School, in Phoenix, Arizona, helps students turn reams into dreams. She and her colleagues prepare information packets that include everything from sample applications to a schedule for filing and following up. Still, the financial aid maze has become so complicated that outside help is often brought in.

"The Phoenix Educational Opportunity Center is very good at assisting us," Smith says. "Representatives visit twice a week, working with students individually or in groups. They also hold financial workshops for parents and students."

There's help from colleges, too. College financial aid officers have become experts at creative finance. They work with parents and students to explain payment plans, loan options, and merit scholarships.

So, if you feel like you might be buried six feet under in paperwork, don't panic. You won't be abandoned.

College First Aid

According to the College Board, student aid for the 1988-89 school year was $26 billion, and about half of all college students received some financial assistance. Let's take a look at how financial aid works, by first defining the terms:

SCHOLARSHIPS AND GRANTS Scholarships and grants—which don't have to be repaid—are available from many sources. These sources include federal and state governments, professional and service organizations, individual schools, private foundations, and corporations. The largest source of direct grant money is the federal Pell Grant Program.

LOANS Student loans from the federal government, also known as Guaranteed Student Loans (GSLs), can be offered through the school or through private financial institutions such as banks, savings & loans, or credit unions. Interest rates on these guaranteed student loans are usually very reasonable. Depending on the program, the money may be lent to you or your parents. And yes, the GSL is really a loan—the money must be paid back!

WORK-STUDY PROGRAMS Many colleges provide jobs for students as part of their financial aid plans. On-campus jobs allow students to earn money toward their education while going to school. You might end up working in the cafeteria, helping maintain the grounds, or cleaning dorms, but the money you make will help pay the costs of receiving an education. You might even find a job related to your program of study.

Who qualifies for a scholarship, loan, or work-study grant? The answer to this question is another question: how much money is available from mom and dad? Don't laugh. This is a critical item in determining your level of financial need, and the aid you may consequently receive. The federal government actually determines the amount of money it expects you and your family to pay toward your education.

How do you apply for these scholarships, loans, and work-study grants? The federal government is a wellspring of money for education. The divining rod for finding that money is the Application for Federal Student Aid (AFSA). Colleges use the responses on this form to determine your specific financial need. The analysis includes many factors, including the size of your family, household living expenses, and even the number of family members attending college. After these expenses have been subtracted from family income, a certain portion is earmarked as the family contribution to your education. This amount, plus any summer earnings you might contribute, is then subtracted from the total cost of your education to determine your level of need.

The Forms

When you apply for federal aid, you can use one of the forms listed below. However, if you want to be considered for non-federal aid, your school may specify which form it wants.

▼ The U.S. Department of Education's
Application for Federal Student Aid (AFSA)

▼ The Pennsylvania Higher Education Assistance Agency's
Application for Pennsylvania State Grants and
Federal Student Aid

▼ The Illinois State Scholarship Commission's
Application for Federal and State Student Aid (AFSSA)

These forms are free. The following services charge for processing the information collected on their forms:

▼ The College Scholarship Service's
Financial Aid Form (FAF)

▼ The American College Testing Program's
Family Financial Statement (FFS)

▼ The Student Aid Application for California (SAAC)

Again, this information should be readily obtainable from your guidance counseling office. However, it can also be obtained from the U.S. Department of Education in its brochure "The Student Guide to Financial Aid from the U.S. Department of Education: Grants, Loans and Work Study."

It is from the results of these applications that many federal programs are made available to the students.

One of these federal programs is the Pell Grant, an award of money that doesn't have to be paid back by the student. Pell Grants are based on financial need.

If you demonstrate sufficient financial need to qualify for a Pell Grant, the amount of money you can receive is based on a number of factors. The first is how much money is available in the pool, which is based on program funding, determined by Congress. Other considerations are whether you're a full- or part-time student, and what the cost of your education is. If you're eligible for a Pell Grant, you will get money. The only question is how much.

Other federal money may come directly from the schools. The most sought-after are Supplemental Education Opportunity Grants, known as SEOGs. You'll have to get an application for SEOG from your school. Like Pell Grants, they don't have to be paid back. This grant can be in addition to any money received from a Pell Grant. But like the dinner table of a big family, it's first-come, first-served, and there's no guarantee that every needy student will be fed. The school only has a finite pool of money, and when it's gone, it's gone.

Under the federal College Work-Study Program (CWS), the college will arrange a job for you to help pay for school. Don't fret about working the cafeteria line; it's a great way to meet people. The school sets the hours, taking into account your schedule, health, and academic progress. Pay is at least minimum wage.

The Perkins Loan is a low-interest loan. You can borrow up to $4,500 if you've completed less than 2 years of a program leading to a bachelor's degree, and $9,000 if you've completed 2 years of undergraduate work. Money is also available for post-graduate studies. But Mr. Perkins (aka Uncle Sam) expects to be paid back. Other loans with a federal blessing are also available.

What happens if you don't pay back your student loan? Some bad things! Your school can require that you repay the entire amount immediately, and it can ask the federal government for help in collecting. The government will inform credit bureaus of your default, affecting your credit ratings. You may find it very difficult to borrow from a bank to buy a car. Also, the IRS can withhold any income tax refunds and apply them toward the loan repayment.

Great States and Merit Scholarships

Diana never anticipated going to college. Her grades in school were strong, but her family was on public assistance. There was absolutely no way she could turn to her parents for financial support. Diana was approached by one of the guidance counselors in her school who was aware of both her family's economic plight and Diana's academic strengths. She was encouraged to apply to the universities in her home state. The total cost would be about $7,000. The federal government had agreed to pay for approximately $3,000 of her annual college expenses and her state government agreed to pitch in another $3,000. Even though Diana had to find another $1,000 through a scholarship or work-study program, she realized that college was in her grasp.

States also pitch in when it comes to handing out money to students. Programs will vary from state to state. Some award money is based on academic achievement only, others strictly on financial need. Often, you must attend a university located within the state to qualify. In other words, you can't use an Illinois State Scholarship to attend the University of Hawaii.

One other financial aid avenue for students to explore is merit scholarships. These awards are usually based on academic achievement and not financial need. According to a survey conducted by the College Board and National Association of Student Financial Aid Administrators, more than 85% of private colleges offer merit scholarships. But merit scholarships may also be offered to students with outstanding achievements in student government, or who have been active in their communities. If you're a very bright, talented, or civic-minded student, you should consider applying for a merit scholarship.

Athlete's Feat

Student athletes may also attend school under a grant-in-aid, more commonly known as an athletic scholarship. Football, basketball, and baseball are the more visible sports, but scholarships are also offered for such sports as cross country, track, fencing, golf, gymnastics, and ice hockey. Skiing, soccer, swimming, lacrosse, and tennis also offer financial aid awards to students.

The best news is that college athletics has recently embraced the woman athlete. In fact, Division I Women's sports sometimes offer more grants-in-aid than the men's sports.

Student-athletes who can play college sports are usually assisted by their high school coaches in turning their athletic abilities into financial aid. Once in school, continued participation in the sport and certain academic standards are required for the grant-in-aid to be renewed. In most cases, if you don't play, the school doesn't pay. However, most schools won't cut off financial aid to injured athletes.

Even late bloomers have a chance. For four years, Bill was the last man to be cut from the high school basketball team. However, he continued to play in church leagues because he loved the sport. His skills improved and he became a great ball-handling guard. When Bill went to college, he half-heartedly tried out for the team. Not only did he make the team, but he was a starter, and received financial aid.

Batteries Included

Sometimes it takes brains, not brawn, to win a scholarship. Sometimes it takes more than brains; it takes a creative spark. Jerry Pratt wanted to go to the Massachusetts Institute of Technology. The problem was that tuition, room & board, and transportation costs would approach $24,000 per year. Quite simply, there wasn't enough family money for him to pay for MIT.

One day at school, Jerry saw a poster for the Duracell National Science Teachers Association Scholarship Competition. "I needed money for college," Jerry recalls, "but I was more intrigued by the challenge. I had to build something that was powered by batteries and then submit it to the Duracell people."

Jerry built the "Knock-Out" Keyless Door Lock. "I used a couple of computer chips, battery-powered of course, to make the 'Knock-Out' lock. The device memorizes a rat-a-tat-tat of a door knock. The door locks to the beat and unlocks to another beat."

The idea was worth $10,000—Jerry won first prize in the Duracell NSTA competition But the $10,000, paid out at $2,500 a year, was still a far cry from the $24,000 he would need.

After receiving Jerry's AFSA, the government determined that Jerry and his family could pay $3,450 toward his education. He was given a Pell Grant of $1,284, plus an SEOG of $4,000. Jerry's stepfather is a disabled Viet Nam veteran, so Jerry was able to qualify for $4,384 in Veteran's Disability money. MIT awarded a further grant of $4,966. A Stafford Loan of $2,450 and Perkins Loan of $1,250 left Jerry about $1,000 short of his funding goal. He works to make up that shortfall.

Here's how it all added up for Jerry:

Duracell NSTA scholarship (annual payment)	$2,500
Pell Grant	$1,284
SEOG	$4,000
Veteran's Disability money	$3,384
MIT Grant	$4,966
Stafford Loan	$2,450
Perkins Loan	$1,250
Family contribution	$3,450
Total	$23,284

Jerry approached his college financing in an organized manner, and he pursued every opportunity. "You've got to believe that the money will come," Jerry says. "But you've got to pursue every lead possible."

"Hot Tips for Cold Cash"

Did you know that tens of millions of dollars in scholarship money were not used last year? Some students simply assumed that they wouldn't qualify. A few were just too lazy to fill out the forms and applications. But for most students, the reason was that they didn't know where to find the money.

But how do you find out about this money? Again, the guidance counseling office should be your first source. You can also go to the library, where you'll find books outlining various scholarship programs and how to apply. You can write to the government. You can dial 1-800-333-INFO, the Federal State Financial Aid Information Center. Or you can call upon the services of an education consultant who helps families hunt for money.

"The NBA offers 58 thousand-dollar scholarships per year to high school seniors for a 500-word essay on the importance of a college education," reports Annette Hubbell. Hubbell is the president of Education Futures, a San Diego-based firm which tracks over $8 billion in private-sector scholarships, grants, and loans from over 30,000 verified sources.

Parents and students use firms like Hubbell's to help find many different forms of financial aid. "Scholarships are the most popular," reports Hubbell. "You never have to pay them back."

Here are some of her "hot tips for cold cash:"

GET GOING Allow six months to a year to begin the process of searching for scholarship money. Two years are better. You have to work around deadlines and response times.

DO YOUR HOMEWORK Treat the search for scholarship money like a major term project. In 1990, the Rotary Club offered $16 million to students who want to study abroad. Minority and ethnic groups award students of those groups scholarships. The National Scholarship Program for Outstanding Negro Students, for example, offers black students up to $2,000 per year in four-year scholarships. If you are a descendant of a Civil War veteran (Union or Confederate), you're eligible for scholarship money.

SAVE EVERYTHING   Hang on to all your homework and school projects; they often can be recycled. Students competing for scholarships are often asked to write a poem or essay. You might need to submit a drawing, or a mechanical device built in an engineering class. By hanging onto these completed assignments, you'll save yourself a great deal of time. Ask your teachers to help in this process. Let them know that you have an essay to write for a scholarship, and ask if you can incorporate it into your current school work.

FOLLOW DIRECTIONS AND BE NEAT   Do exactly what you're asked to do. If the application must be typed, then type it. Applications that do not conform to simple instructions are not even considered.

KEEP A SCHEDULE   Keep a list of deadlines and goals so you can keep track of what's due when. Again, this sounds simple, but it works.

"You don't have to be a jock or a genius or even be poor to qualify for a scholarship these days," Hubbell reports. "Many are awarded for volunteer efforts, career choice, ethnic background, or simply because no one else applied!"

Over 31% of all first year college expenses are paid by scholarships. Shouldn't you be getting your fair share?

Three Hots and a Cot

On television, hungry teenagers unable to pay for college discover that by joining the Armed Forces (Army, Navy, Air Force, Coast Guard, or Marines), they can put money away for their college educations. You put $1,200 away, and at the end of a four-year enlistment, you could have $25,200 set aside for your college education.

The other military option is ROTC, NROTC, or one of the service academies. West Point, Annapolis, King's Point, and the Air Force Academy not only offer full four-year scholarships, but their students are paid half the salary of a second lieutenant or ensign. You also have a job guarantee upon graduation. Service academy graduates are required to serve for 6 years.

You must apply for an ROTC or NROTC scholarship. Service academy candidates are sponsored by a congressional representative, a senator, the Secretary of the Navy, the Secretary of Defense, the Vice President, or the President. Children of Congressional Medal of Honor winners enjoy preferential status in gaining admission. But the door is open to everyone.

By planning ahead, by treating the search for money as a job, by keeping a schedule, and by demonstrating "stick-to-it-iveness," you can find a way to pay for school. And the best time to start this search is NOW!